W9-ARM-907

MAINE
Acadia

Voyageurs

Pictured Rocks

NEW HAMPSHIRE
White Mountain

VERMONT
Marsh-Billings-Rockefeller

MASSACHUSETTS
Lowell

Saratoga

MICHIGAN

MINNESOTA

Apostle Islands

WISCONSIN

NEW YORK

RHODE ISLAND
Block Island

NEW JERSEY
Ellis Island

PENNSYLVANIA
Gettysburg

CONNECTICUT
Weir Farm

Effigy Mounds

IOWA

Perry's Victory

Cuyahoga Valley

OHIO

INDIANA

ILLINOIS

George Rogers Clark

Harper's Ferry

WEST VIRGINIA

DELAWARE
Bombay Hook

MARYLAND
Fort McHenry

Shenandoah

VIRGINIA

Shawnee

KENTUCKY
Cumberland Gap

DISTRICT OF COLUMBIA
Frederick Douglass

MISSOURI

Ozark

Great Smoky Mountains

NORTH CAROLINA

Blue Ridge

TENNESSEE

SOUTH CAROLINA

ARKANSAS
Hot Springs

Tuskegee Airmen

GEORGIA

Fort Sumter
Cumberland Island

MISSISSIPPI
Vicksburg

ALABAMA

Kisatchie

FLORIDA

Castillo de San Marcos

LOUISIANA

Everglades

AMERICAN SAMOA

National Park of American Samoa

El Yunque

PUERTO RICO

U.S. VIRGIN ISLANDS

Salt River Bay

Jacqueline Anderson
1140 E Mishawaka Ave
Mishawaka, IN 46544

Jacqueline Anderson
1140 E Mishawaka Ave
Mishawaka, IN 46544

National
PARKS

A Kid's Guide to America's Parks, Monuments, and Landmarks

The National Park poster series in this book were originally produced between 1938 and 1941. The artists and actual
dates of production are unknown although it is thought that many were the work of "Chester" Don Powell, a
California WPA artist. The original posters were distributed to local Chambers of Commerce to advertise parks
and were not for sale. This series all but disappeared for nearly 35 years until one poster was pulled from the park
burn pile in Grand Teton National Park in 1973. Another 20 years elapsed until a black and white photograph
collection of these posters was discovered in a file drawer in Harper's Ferry West Virginia. Using the original Grand
Teton poster as a template and the black and white photographs, this unique poster collection was restored—
each screen painstakingly hand drawn. Since completion of the original 14 posters, many parks have requested new
park images in this style. These contemporary posters were created by Brian Maebius and Doug Leen.
For more information, visit www.rangerdoug.com.

Published by
Black Dog & Leventhal Publishers, Inc.
151 West 19th Street
New York, NY 10011

Distributed by
Workman Publishing Company
225 Varick Street
New York, NY 10014

Manufactured in China

Cover and interior design by Red Herring Design

ISBN-13: 978-1-57912-884-5

h g f e d c b

Library of Congress Cataloging-in-Publication Data

National PARKS

A Kid's Guide to America's Parks, Monuments, and Landmarks

ERIN McHUGH

ART BY NEAL ASPINALL, DOUG LEEN, AND BRIAN MAEBIUS

BLACK DOG
& LEVENTHAL
PUBLISHERS
NEW YORK

TABLE OF CONTENTS

INTRODUCTION

Teddy Roosevelt and
John Muir, Yosemite 1906

❝As long as I live, I'll hear waterfalls and bird and winds sing. I'll interpret the rocks, learn the language of flood, storm and avalanche. I'll acquaint myself with the glaciers and wild gardens, and get as near the heart of the world as I can.❞ —JOHN MUIR

J ohn Muir was one of the first people to propose the idea of preserving wilderness in the United States. In 1868, he moved into a small cabin on the Yosemite Creek and fell in love with the area. His enthusiasm and vivid descriptions of its beauty helped make it a national park in 1890. He often served as a guide.

One person who joined Muir at Yosemite was President Theodore Roosevelt. Always an eager student of nature, Roosevelt spent years as a cowboy on his ranch in the Badlands of North Dakota. While president, he camped with Muir in Yosemite for three days in 1903. Roosevelt went on to add five national parks during his presidency, including Crater Lake and Mesa Verde.

These are just two of the dedicated people who helped create 58 national parks, 100 national monuments, and more than 2,400 national historic landmarks in the United States. The United States was the first country in the entire world to establish a national park system, and this book profiles more than 75 of these parks alphabetically by state, from the rocky shores of Maine's Acadia National Park to the ancient redwood groves of northern California. Along the way you'll learn about the wonders to be found there, such as the General Sherman Giant Sequoia in California that is 2,700 years old and the bison at Yellowstone that can run up to 30 mph!

But not all of our parks are sprawling wilderness, and you'll also learn about some of America's surprising and important historic spots, too: parks that honor the early days of the cotton mills, forts, airfields, artists' colonies, World War II Pacific Ocean war sites, famous battlegrounds, beautiful highways, and so much more—even a prison.

A famous author named Wallace Stegner once called our national parks "America's best idea." After you read this book, we think you'll agree!

TUSKEGEE AIRMEN
NATIONAL HISTORIC SITE

This tiny park tells a huge story in America's history. Until the latter half of the twentieth century, soldiers were traditionally segregated by race when they served their country. One notable exception took place right here in Tuskegee, Alabama.

The government believed that African-Americans weren't qualified for the rigors of piloting a fighter jet until the Army Air Corps gave them a chance. By the late 1930s, suspecting that World War II was at hand and that many more pilots would be needed, the Tuskegee Experiment was born. The perfect place to set up this program was at the Tuskegee Institute, a small black college with an aeronautical engineering program started by the famous educator Booker T. Washington. The institute already had instructors and facilities, and the warm weather was perfect for year-round training. They taught not only airmen but mechanics, navigators, and support staff. The Tuskegee Airmen subsequently became some of the most respected fighter pilots of World War II.

Now here, at Moton Field, on the same spot where they all trained, is the Hangar One Museum with an array of World War II–era planes. You can also listen to recorded oral history in the airmen's own voices.

RANGER FACT

In 2007, President George W. Bush presented the Congressional Medal of Honor to more than 300 living Tuskegee Airmen or their wives.

AMAZING BUT TRUE!

In 1941, First Lady Eleanor Roosevelt showed Americans exactly what she thought of the Tuskegee Airmen: Despite the Secret Service's objections, she went up on a flight with one of them.

OTHER NATIONAL PARKS IN ALABAMA

Horseshoe Bend
NATIONAL MILITARY PARK

Little River Canyon
NATIONAL PRESERVE

Natchez Trace PARKWAY

Russell Cave NATIONAL MONUMENT

Selma to Montgomery
NATIONAL HISTORIC TRAIL

Trail of Tears
NATIONAL HISTORIC TRAIL

By the Numbers

1998: Year park was established

89.69: Acres in the park

10,000: Approximate number of visitors per year

16,000: People trained here between 1941 and 1946

150: Distinguished Flying Crosses earned

1,578: Missions completed

> "You caused America to look in the mirror of its soul and you showed America that there was nothing a black person couldn't do."
>
> —COLIN POWELL, *a retired U.S. Army general and former secretary of state, to the airmen*

ALASKA

RANGER NATURALIST SERVICE

VISIT NORTH AMERICA'S HIGHEST MOUNTAIN — 20,320 FEET

MOUNT McKINLEY
NATIONAL PARK

U.S. DEPARTMENT
OF THE INTERIOR

EST 1917

NATIONAL PARK
SERVICE

DENALI
NATIONAL PARK

Think big—*really* big. The entire Denali National Park and Preserve is bigger than the state of Massachusetts! It includes the Alaska Range, with the famous Mount McKinley named after William McKinley, the twenty-fifth president of the United States.

Alaskans prefer to call the mountain Denali, meaning the "High One," which makes sense since it is the highest peak in North America. Believe it or not, the youngest person to climb to the summit was only eleven years old!

The animal life may be the most exciting thing about Denali. It is the only national park patrolled by sled dogs. The park has more than three dozen species of mammals—from grizzly and black bears, caribou, moose, gray wolf and wolverines, to foxes, lynx, and Dall sheep—but no reptiles due to the cold temperatures. This also slows down the metabolism of the fish, so they're smaller than you'd find in other places.

Plant life is unusual, too. Because of its subarctic landscape, there are lots of fungi, algae, mosses, and lichen growing in the colder and shadier places. But you'll also see beautiful plants that flower in the short summer months, like lupine, bluebell, goldenrod, and fireweed.

AMAZING BUT TRUE!

On June 21, the longest day of the year, there are almost twenty-one hours of sunlight here. But on the shortest day, December 21? Just a little more than four hours!

RANGER FACT

Approximately 30 huskies log 3,000 miles patrolling the park during the winter. In the summer, they give daily sled demonstrations that have been seen by nearly 50,000 people a year!

the GREAT AMERICAN BIRDWATCH

GYRFALCON

The Gyrfalcon sounds like something imaginary out of Harry Potter, but it's actually the largest of the falcon species living on Arctic coasts. The female is bigger than the male, and can grow more than two feet long, with a wingspan of over five feet. From snowy white to dark brown, they are often used for hunting and falconry.

By the Numbers

1980: Year park was established

1,760: Square miles in the park

285,000+: Approximate number of visitors per year

800: Inches of snow the Harding Icefield often receives each year

38: Glaciers in the park

20: Species of seabirds that nest by the thousands on the rocky crags of the fjords

117: Miles per hour wind gusts recorded in the park

3: Categories of "killer whales" seen in the park

KENAI FJORDS
NATIONAL PARK

When we think of fjords, they seem as foreign as they sound—faraway and somewhat Scandinavian. But fjords are actually inlets with very steep sides, and sea water flowing through the valley between them. As they are formed by longtime glacial activity, it's not surprising to find them in a national park in Alaska.

KENAI FJORDS
NATIONAL PARK

Hand in hand with fjords, of course, are the glaciers that created them. At Kenai Fjords, you can get close to the incredible Exit Glacier. It is a valley glacier, which is a moving river of ice. The Exit Glacier flows about ten inches a day from the Harding Icefield. Beyond glaciers there is a rainforest, alpine tundra, and the coast.

But the wildlife is as big a draw here as the landscape: You can take a boat tour with a ranger and spot sea lions, puffins, sea otters, porpoises, seals, and the most spectacular sighting of all, humpback and orca whales. Look toward land and you might even see some mountain goats! There is kayaking here for the very experienced, and some stalwart adventurers will tackle the backcountry, camping, kayaking, and trekking across hundreds of thousands of pristine acres.

AMAZING BUT TRUE!

Harding Icefield, which is in the park, is the only icefield totally within the United States—and it covers more than three hundred square miles!

the
GREAT AMERICAN BIRDWATCH

TUFTED PUFFIN

Found primarily in the North Pacific Ocean, the Tufted Puffin is known for the yellow tufts on its head, its thick red bill and feet, and its mostly black body. They nest in burrows on cliffs close to the water, away from predators and with easy access to the water. Some of these burrows can be 5 feet deep.

OTHER NATIONAL PARKS In ALASKA

Alagnak WILD RIVER

Aleutian World War II NATIONAL HISTORIC AREA

Aniakchak NATIONAL MONUMENT & PRESERVE

Bering Land Bridge NATIONAL PRESERVE

Cape Krusenstern NATIONAL MONUMENT

Gates of the Arctic NATIONAL PARK & PRESERVE

Glacier Bay NATIONAL PARK & PRESERVE

Inupiat HERITAGE CENTER

Katmai NATIONAL PARK & PRESERVE

Klondike Gold Rush NATIONAL HISTORICAL PARK

Kobuk Valley NATIONAL PARK

Lake Clark NATIONAL PARK & PRESERVE

Noatak NATIONAL PRESERVE

Sitka NATIONAL HISTORICAL PARK

USS Arizona MEMORIAL

Western Arctic NATIONAL PARKLANDS

Wrangell-St. Elias NATIONAL PARK & PRESERVE

Yukon-Charley Rivers NATIONAL PRESERVE

By the Numbers

1988: Year park was established

10,500: Acres in the park

3,900: Visitors per year

3,000: Years ago people came here by sea from Southeast Asia

200+: Types of coral in the park

890: Species of fish on reef

59° F: Lowest recorded temperature (1964)

11,000: Miles round-trip some birds fly from Alaska to American Samoa annually

AMAZING BUT TRUE!

About half the tuna you find on the grocery shelf comes from American Samoa canneries.

NATIONAL PARK OF AMERICAN SAMOA

There are so many unusual things about this park, not the least of which is that it's the only U.S. national park south of the equator.

American Samoa is in the South Pacific, about 2,300 miles southwest of Hawaii. It consists of several beautiful islands that are filled with rain forests and surrounded by coral reefs. This means lots of hiking, scuba diving, and fantastic snorkeling. And if you're interested in unusual animals, there are humpback whales, colorful tropical fish, geckos, and even the flying fox, which is actually a fruit bat with a wingspan of three feet. As for the plants, about 30 percent of the plant life, which is almost five hundred plants and ferns, are only found on these islands.

You can hike a trail to the top of a mountain, see some World War II gun battlements, and swim with the turtles—all in the same day!

RANGER FACT

American Samoa is the southernmost territory in the United States, and is only slightly bigger than Washington, D.C.

The GREAT AMERICAN BIRDWATCH

BROWN BOOBY

It's no surprise that seabirds like the Booby are prevalent around American Samoa. About thirty inches long with a white belly, they are fliers whose talents lie in pinpoint diving, not in taking off or landing. The Booby catches food at the ocean's surface, and can even pick a leaping fish out of the air.

13

By the Numbers

1919: Year park was established

5,000,000: visitors every year

105° F: Highest temperature on the South Rim (1974)

160: Number of rapids in the Colorado River

100: Inches of snow a year on the North Rim, which is **1,000** feet higher than the South Rim

5: Indian tribes that live in the Canyon—the Hopi, Navajo, Havasupai, Paiute and Hualapai

A FREE GOVERNMENT SERVICE
GRAND CANYON
NATIONAL PARK
U.S. DEPARTMENT OF THE INTERIOR

EST 1919

NATIONAL PARK SERVICE

GRAND CANYON

NATIONAL PARK

This is one of the most famous of our national parks, and no wonder. When you get to the rim of the Grand Canyon for the first time, the size and beauty make your jaw drop. And yet, even though it was given federal protection by our government way back in 1893, this didn't become part of the park system until 1919. That year, 44,173 people came and visited: That's a lot, considering there were no planes and very few cars or highways to bring them here.

RANGER FACT

The Grand Canyon is known as one of the Seven Natural Wonders of the World.

But the years since its establishment as a national park are a blink of the eye when you think of how long it took to create this canyon. The Grand Canyon began forming about seventeen million years ago through erosion caused by the Colorado River. That river, which is about six thousand feet below the South Rim, etched its way through the rocks to create a canyon that is 277 miles long and as wide as 18 miles.

In the deepest part of the Canyon, the Colorado River flows past rocks that are 1.8 billion years old.

There are many great ways to see the canyon: People fly over in planes and helicopters, hike to the bottom, or even ride a donkey down the trails. But white-water rafting is one of the most spectacular. Today there are guides and sophisticated rafts to take you. It was not so easy in 1869, on the expedition led by geologist John Wesley Powell: His was the first passage through the canyon by European Americans. Even though Powell had lost one arm in the Civil War, he was a very brave explorer. Some of the nine other men and four boats in his party did not return from the expedition with Powell, but their trip gave us

invaluable information about both the Colorado River and the Grand Canyon.

Plant and animal life changes dramatically in the canyon, depending on the depth from the rim. Bats, rodents, fungi, and lichen are abundant here; mammals range from porcupines to black bear, and, of course, lots of snakes! Look overhead and you may even see a rare California condor. Top to bottom, it's one of our greatest national parks.

> 66 **The Grand Canyon fills me with awe. It is beyond comparison — beyond description; absolutely unparalleled throughout the wide world.** 99
>
> **—PRESIDENT THEODORE ROOSEVELT**
> *a champion of the Nations Park system, as he stood on the rim of the Grand Canyon in 1903*

the GREAT AMERICAN BIRDWATCH

CALIFORNIA CONDOR

The condor has the largest wingspan of any bird found in North America (up to 9 1/2 feet) and is one of the heaviest (18–23 pounds). It is also one of the world's longest-living birds (up to 50 years).

The skin of its bald head changes from yellow to bright red, depending on the bird's mood. As of 2010, there were 381 condors known to be living, including 192 in the wild.

1994: Year park was established, though a national monument in 1933

115° F: Highest temperature recorded (1994)

600,000: Visitors a year

12: Inches of rainfall each year

200: Gallons of water the saguaro's shallow roots can collect each rainfall

40 million: Seeds each saguaro can produce during its lifetime

100: Flowers may appear on a single saguaro

16,000: Weight, in pounds, of a large, well-hydrated saguaro, which is typically **85** percent water

6: Species of rattlesnake found in the park

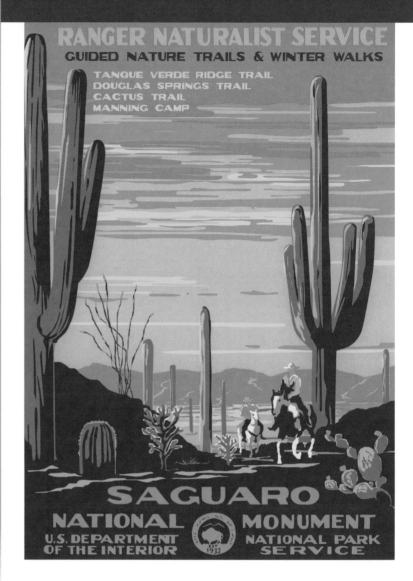

RANGER NATURALIST SERVICE
GUIDED NATURE TRAILS & WINTER WALKS
TANQUE VERDE RIDGE TRAIL
DOUGLAS SPRINGS TRAIL
CACTUS TRAIL
MANNING CAMP

SAGUARO
NATIONAL MONUMENT
U.S. DEPARTMENT OF THE INTERIOR
EST. 1933
NATIONAL PARK SERVICE

SAGUARO
NATIONAL PARK

The park's original name, Saguaro National Monument, is a rather weird choice for a name, because there is no actual monument here. On the other hand, the saguaro cactus, after which it was named, is something of a monument among cactuses. In fact, the world's largest cactus, called the "Grand One"—a saguaro, of course—was burned in a fire a few years ago. It was forty-six feet tall, and nearly two hundred years old! And a cool thing about the saguaro blossom—which is Arizona's state flower, by the way—it opens at night, in the dark, and blooms for less than twenty-four hours before it dies.

RANGER FACT

Bet you think saguaros must grow pretty fast to get this big, but in the first several years, they only grow about an inch to an inch and a half!

The park is unusual in other ways: It covers nearly 100,000 acres of almost complete wilderness, and is divided into two parts in the Sonoran Desert—on two sides of the city of Tucson.

Animals that live in the desert heat don't have an easy life, so only the most adaptable ones survive. Lots of bats, which like to come out at night when it's cool; hummingbirds and bees, which actually make their home inside the holes of the saguaro, like birdhouses; and, maybe cleverest of all, vultures: They actually urinate on themselves to cool off!

PETRIFIED
FOREST
NATIONAL PARK

Cacti are awesome—no doubt about it. But so are trees, especially when they're petrified. The trees in this park were fossilized about 225 million years ago by volcanic ash, which then turned into quartz crystals—which is how they get their color. More than twelve tons of petrified wood disappear in tourists' pockets and cars every year from this park, taken home as souvenirs.

The changing geography also left something else in the park: the fossils of amphibians, giant reptiles, and even early dinosaurs. The Petrified Forest is part of Arizona's Painted Desert, named by the Spanish explorers for its unusual colors: You'll see orange, pink, red, and other hues, a result of large deposits of iron and manganese in the sand, formed into layers over the centuries.

We believe that people lived here as far back as eight thousand years ago, and were growing crops like corn upwards of two thousand years ago. Soon after that, these people built pueblos (villages) to live in together, and you'll see traces of some of them here still.

And the animals! Jackrabbits, coyotes, prairie dogs living in colonies that are like towns, bobcats, and pronghorns—which are antelopelike creatures that are the fastest animals on the continent, sprinting through the desert at up to sixty miles per hour.

AMAZING BUT TRUE!

The original Route 66 went right through the Petrified Forest. Built in 1926, it started in Chicago, Illinois and ended near Los Angeles, California.

PETRIFIED FOREST
NATIONAL MONUMENT

FREE GUIDE AND LECTURE SERVICE
AT THE
RAINBOW FOREST MUSEUM
DAILY-EVERY HOUR ON THE HOUR
8 AM TO 4 PM

U.S. DEPARTMENT OF THE INTERIOR
NATIONAL PARK SERVICE
MADE BY WPA · C.C.C

By the Numbers

1962: Year park was established (named a National Monument in 1906)

600,000: Visitors a year

66: Name of famous highway (Route 66) that passes through the park

3: Minerals (pure quartz, manganese oxide, and iron oxide) that make up the main colors of the petrified wood

200: Species of birds in the park

OTHER NATIONAL PARKS In ARIZONA

Canyon de Chelly
NATIONAL MONUMENT

Casa Grande Ruins
NATIONAL MONUMENT

Chiricahua NATIONAL MONUMENT

Coronado NATIONAL MEMORIAL

Glen Canyon
NATIONAL RECREATION AREA

Hohokam Pima NATIONAL MONUMENT

Hubbell Trading Post
NATIONAL HISTORIC SITE

Juan Bautista de Anza
NATIONAL HISTORIC TRAIL

Lake Mead
NATIONAL RECREATION AREA

Montezuma Castle
NATIONAL MONUMENT

Navajo NATIONAL MONUMENT

Old Spanish NATIONAL HISTORIC TRAIL

Organ Pipe Cactus
NATIONAL MONUMENT

Pipe Spring NATIONAL MONUMENT

Sunset Crater Volcano
NATIONAL MONUMENT

Tonto NATIONAL MONUMENT

Tumacacori NATIONAL HISTORICAL PARK

Tuzigoot NATIONAL MONUMENT

Walnut Canyon NATIONAL MONUMENT

Wupatki NATIONAL MONUMENT

Yuma Crossing
NATIONAL HERITAGE AREA

By the Numbers

1921: Year park was established

5,500: Acres in the park, making it one of the smallest national parks in the country

1,200,000: Visitors each year

700,000: Gallons of water that flow from the springs each day into pipes and a reservoir system

143° F: Temperature in the springs

98: Length of Bridge Street (in feet), where the "World's Shortest St. Patrick's Day Parade" is held annually

AMAZING BUT TRUE!
The hot water you enjoy in the springs starts the heating process a mile below ground!

HOT SPRINGS NATIONAL PARK

Today when you hear the word *spa,* you think of massages and manicures and saunas. But Hot Springs has been known as the American Spa since the 1800s, when people came here to "take the waters." What does that mean? The natural springs here are rich in minerals and heated underground by the earth's crust. Both then and now, visitors drink the water for good health, and relax in pools to cure illness and relieve pain. In fact, up until the 1940s, lots of major league baseball teams brought their players here to soothe their aches and sore muscles. In those days, many people stayed several months!

RANGER FACT

The very first National Park Ranger killed in the line of duty worked here. James Cary was shot by bootleggers smuggling liquor in 1927, during Prohibition.

Though Hot Springs is all about the waters, make no mistake: Animals galore roam throughout the nation's smallest national park. Since the area is highly populated with people, you won't find large prey around, but there are plenty of bats and rodents, salamanders, frogs, and even eels. And birds like the mild climate here as well: You might spy anything from a tiny hummingbird to a great blue heron, cuckoos to wild turkeys, running around.

There's hiking, camping, and picnicking here at Hot Springs, but the best place to start your exploring is at the Fordyce Bath House, a beautiful old building that was one of the original spas, and now serves as a visitors' center. It's right in town, because the town of Hot Springs, Arkansas actually grew up around the spa. In fact, it's the only national park that has a town *inside* it!

OTHER NATIONAL PARKS In ARKANSAS

Arkansas Post
NATIONAL MEMORIAL

Buffalo NATIONAL RIVER

Fort Smith
NATIONAL HISTORIC SITE

Little Rock Central High School
NATIONAL HISTORIC SITE

Pea Ridge
NATIONAL MILITARY PARK

President William Jefferson Clinton Birthplace Home
NATIONAL HISTORIC SITE

Trail of Tears
NATIONAL HISTORIC TRAIL

the GREAT AMERICAN BIRDWATCH

GREAT HORNED OWL

This owl's distinctive "horns" are neither ears nor horns, simply tufts of feathers. Great Horned Owls range in length from eighteen to twenty-five inches, and have a wingspan of forty to sixty inches. Their call is a low-pitched but loud *ho-ho-hoo hoo hoo.* Their eyes are nearly as large as those of humans. They have two hundred to three hundred pounds per square inch of crushing power in their talons, compared with the human grip strength of twenty pounds per square inch.

CALIFORNIA

RANGER NATURALIST SERVICE

HEADQUARTERS YOSEMITE MUSEUM

AUTO CARAVANS
NATURE WALKS
MUSEUM LECTURES
ILLUSTRATED TALKS
ALL-DAY HIKES
CAMP-FIRE PROGRAMS
SEVEN-DAY HIKES
JUNIOR NATURE SCHOOL
WILDFLOWER GARDEN
INDIAN DEMONSTRATIONS
NATURALIST STATIONED AT
MARIPOSA GROVE MUSEUM,
GLACIER POINT, AND
TUOLUMNE MEADOWS

YOSEMITE
NATIONAL PARK

EST 1890

U.S. DEPARTMENT
OF THE INTERIOR

NATIONAL PARK
SERVICE

The GREAT AMERICAN BIRDWATCH

AMERICAN DIPPER

The American Dipper is true to its name: it catches all of its food underwater by swimming or walking on the stream bottom, dipping its head up to 60 times a minute to catch insects and fish. Its nasal flaps allow it to stay underwater longer than any songbird—up to thirty

YOSEMITE
NATIONAL PARK

Yosemite is one of America's most popular, beautiful, and visited parks. Although it is massive, most visitors spend their time within just seven square miles! Yosemite is what's known as a wilderness park—about 95 percent of it is untamed land. People started visiting here way back in the 1860s after four men traveled through what would become Yosemite and started writing magazine articles about its grandeur. Imagine: no cars or phones—even the railroad was brand-new.

Yosemite Valley is where most folks come, and here they see stunning views of steep granite cliffs and five of the world's ten highest waterfalls. Spring, when the winter's snows are melting, provides the greatest views and huge, rushing waters. And thousands come to climb those cliffs—Yosemite is one of the great rock-climbing destinations in the world.

So many parts of Yosemite are completely different from one another that it's sometimes hard to believe you're still in the same park: from the glacier-formed valleys to lovely meadows and snowy, alpine peaks at the higher elevations. Of course, that means you'll find different kinds of plants and animals wherever you travel—from mountain beavers and Yosemite toads in the meadows to white-tailed jack-

RANGER FACT

The famous ranger hat, with its unusual "Montana Peak" shape, was first adopted at Yosemite in 1899 when the cavalry was stationed here. It's really a Stetson reshaped to help protect rangers from the rain.

rabbits and yellow-bellied marmots, which can stand the cold and thinner air at heights of more than thirteen thousand feet. In Yosemite Valley itself, you may even see tarantulas!

> ❝ It is by far the grandest of all the special temples of Nature I was ever permitted to enter. ❞
> —JOHN MUIR, *naturalist*

21

KING'S CANYON NATIONAL PARK

This park was once called the General Grant National Park after Ulysses S. Grant, who went on to become the eighteenth president of the United States. Within the park is a giant sequoia tree named after him: The General Grant tree is nearly two thousand years old.

But the majority of the park is known for its canyons and caves. Originally it was thought that Kings Canyon was formed by earthquakes, but famed naturalist John Muir theorized that the Ice Age and its glaciers had carved out this spectacular landscape. There are caves at the bottom of these canyons, and Boyden Cave is open for tours in the summer months—you can visit a real "bat cave," called the Bat Grotto, where these flying mammals sleep all day long.

By the Numbers

1940: Year park was established

461,901: Acres in the park

570,000+: Approximate number of visitors each year

17° F: Lowest recorded temperature (1990)

114° F: Highest recorded temperature (1996)

8,200: Depth (in feet) of Kings River Canyon, the deepest canyon in the United States

AMAZING BUT TRUE!

A logger named Walter Fry spent five days with a crew cutting down one sequoia in 1888. When they counted the rings, and he realized they had destroyed a 3,266-year-old tree, he became dedicated to saving these trees.

the GREAT AMERICAN BIRDWATCH

BROWN-HEADED COWBIRD

The Brown-Headed Cowbird is seen in great numbers in the park; it is a parasite, laying its eggs in the nests of other birds. The cowbird got its name from its habit of following large animals, like bison, cows, and horses, to feast on insects their hooves dug up.

GENERAL GRANT TREE 268 FEET TALL

ALSO TOUR SCENIC KINGS CANYON

107 FEET CIRCUMFERENCE AT BASE

GENERAL GRANT NATIONAL PARK
U.S. DEPARTMENT OF THE INTERIOR
NATIONAL PARK SERVICE
EST 1890

SEE GIANT SEQUOIAS
AND THE GENERAL SHERMAN TREE • THE WORLD'S LARGEST

SEQUOIA
NATIONAL PARK
DEPARTMENT THE INTERIOR NATIONAL PARK SERVICE

the
GREAT AMERICAN
BIRDWATCH
WILLOW FLYCATCHER

The olive-brown Willow Flycatcher has long been an inhabitant of the Sierra Nevada. These birds sit at the top of a bush or shrub, and feed by making speedy take-offs to catch insects in flight! Though these creatures are still prevalent, the use of pesticides has taken its toll on the flycatchers' numbers.

SEQUOIA
NATIONAL PARK

SEQUOIA NATIONAL PARK
1939

Kings Canyon and Sequoia National Parks are adjacent to each other, in the Sierra Nevada ("snowy mountain range" in Spanish), and the Generals Highway connects the two. Snow, ice, rain—anything can happen in the parks, and will often force the highway to close on a moment's notice.

Mount Whitney, at 14,505 feet, is the tallest peak in the United States outside of Alaska and Hawaii. It's so high that it is considered alpine: Some of it is above the tree line. This means very few plants and animals can survive there, and the few you might find, like the parnassius phoegus butterfly, or the gray-crowned rosy finch, are just passing through.

But the highlight of the park is the sequoia trees themselves. They are the world's largest and oldest trees, and the General Sherman tree here is the largest tree in the world: It's nearly 275 feet tall and the diameter of the trunk at its base is 36 1/2 feet.

RANGER FACT

The California state flag features a likeness of the grizzly bear—though there are none to be found in the state. But there are plenty of American black bears in Sequoia and Kings Canyon, and you'll find they have black, brown, and even blond fur.

By the
Numbers

1890: Year park was established

404,051: Acres in the park

930,000+: Approximate number of visitors each year

2,700 years: Approximate age of the General Sherman sequoia

300: Distance (in feet) you should stay away from bears

LASSEN VOLCANIC
NATIONAL PARK

Lassen Volcanic National Park has just what you'd expect: volcanoes! There are four different types in the world, and you'll find every one of them here: shield, lava dome, composite, and cinder cone volcanoes.

The area wasn't always oozing lava. In 1914 Lassen Peak began spewing steam and ash in more than 150 eruptions. A year later, the mountaintop exploded with rivers of lava, and continued steaming until 1917. Outside of volcanoes, the park is home to the unusual: the bald eagle, great swarms of the California tortoise shell butterfly, and the smelowskia, a tiny white flower found only here.

By the Numbers

1916: Year park was established

106,000: Acres in the park

400,000: Approximate number of visitors each year

14: Permanent snowfields

100° F: Highest recorded temperature (1981)

−9° F: Lowest recorded temperature (1972)

200: Miles of volcanic ash was spewed during the 1915 eruption of Lassen Peak

OTHER
NATIONAL PARKS |||||||||||| In ||||||||||||
CALIFORNIA

Cabrillo NATIONAL MONUMENT
California NATIONAL HISTORIC TRAIL
Channel Islands NATIONAL PARK
Devils Postpile NATIONAL MONUMENT
Eugene O'Neill NATIONAL HISTORIC SITE
Fort Point NATIONAL HISTORIC SITE
Golden Gate NATIONAL RECREATION AREA
John Muir NATIONAL HISTORIC SITE
Joshua Tree NATIONAL PARK
Lava Beds NATIONAL MONUMENT
Manzanar NATIONAL HISTORIC SITE
Mojave NATIONAL PRESERVE
Muir Woods NATIONAL MONUMENT
Pinnacles NATIONAL MONUMENT
Point Reyes NATIONAL SEASHORE
Pony Express NATIONAL HISTORIC TRAIL
Redwood NATIONAL AND STATE PARKS
Rosie the Riveter/ World War II Home Front NATIONAL HISTORICAL PARK
San Francisco Maritime NATIONAL HISTORICAL PARK
Santa Monica Mountains NATIONAL RECREATION AREA
Whiskeytown-Shasta-Trinity NATIONAL RECREATION AREA

DEATH VALLEY
NATIONAL PARK

Just east of the Sierra Nevada lies Death Valley, which got its name in 1849 when a group of men used it as a shortcut during the California Gold Rush and got lost.

And no wonder—it's both the driest and hottest of our national parks, and 95 percent of the entire park is considered wilderness. Still, there's fun to be had here: You can go sand-sledding on Mesquite Flat Sand Dunes! Also, the wide open spaces here make it one of the darkest places in the country at night, and because of that, Death Valley has some of the best stargazing to be found.

By the Numbers

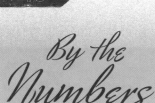

1994: Year park was established

4,774: Acres in the park

770,000: Approximate number of visitors each year

-282 feet: Below sea level of Badwater Basin

153 : Days in a row in 2001 of temperatures above 100° F

GREAT SAND DUNES
NATIONAL PARK AND PRESERVE

Colorado is for skiing, right? That's just what people here do on the sand dunes. And not just any sand dunes—at 750 feet, these are the tallest in the country. Formed by the Rio Grande River, they are thought to be 12,000 years old and change shape daily due to the wind. You can slide, ski or sled down 300' tall slopes. Bordering the dunes is Medano Creek—filled with water that is actually snowmelt— where people swim and build sandcastles.

The Great Sand Dunes is unusually diverse in its geology, and its plant and animal life. Beyond the dunes, there are forests, snow-topped mountains, grasslands and wetlands. There are even six different insects native only to the park, the most famous being the aptly named great sand dunes tiger beetle. At the highest point in the park is alpine tundra, where cold temperatures prevent much plant growth, and only hardier animals, like bighorn sheep, the furry pika, and the marmot, can survive.

RANGER FACT

There are several dunefields here in the park, but the largest one covers thirty square miles!

The GREAT AMERICAN BIRDWATCH
PTARMIGAN

The Ptarmigan is a bird that looks like a chicken and would rather walk than fly! Ptarmigans live in the Great Sand Dunes tundras, and hide out in snowbanks during a blizzard.

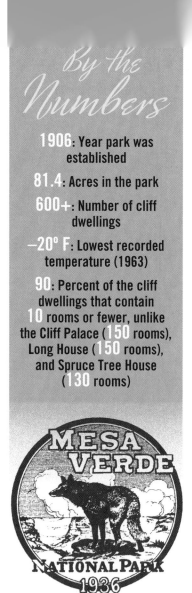

1906: Year park was established

81.4: Acres in the park

600+: Number of cliff dwellings

–20° F: Lowest recorded temperature (1963)

90: Percent of the cliff dwellings that contain **10** rooms or fewer, unlike the Cliff Palace (**150** rooms), Long House (**150** rooms), and Spruce Tree House (**130** rooms)

MESA VERDE NATIONAL PARK 1936

VISIT THE WORLD FAMOUS **CLIFF DWELLINGS** WITH OUR COMPETENT RANGER NATURALIST GUIDES

SQUARE TOWER ALSO CLIFF PALACE BALCONY HOUSE SPRUCE TREE HOUSE SUN TEMPLE OAK TREE HOUSE

• HORSEBACK AND HIKING TRIPS
• PETROGLYPH AND PICTOGRAPH VIEWING
• CAMPFIRE PROGRAMS BY THE SUPERINTENDENT

FREE PUBLIC CAMPGROUNDS **MESA VERDE NATIONAL PARK** U.S. DEPARTMENT OF THE INTERIOR NATIONAL PARK SERVICE

MESA VERDE
NATIONAL PARK

Imagine if the only way people in the future could learn about our lives now was from our houses and the crafts we made. Well, that's what's happened to the Ancient Pueblo people.

At the Mesa Verde park, you'll see some 600 well-preserved Anaszi homes—the cliff dwellings of these Puebloans built between 550–1300 CE. They were usually built in caves or under rock overhangs for protection, and made of pieces of sandstone, packed together with adobe. The largest, called the Cliff Palace, has more than 150 rooms. The men farmed corn and the women made pottery and wove incredible baskets; they even waterproofed their baskets so they could cook in them.

RANGER FACT

Ancient Pueblo pottery is specific to both its time and place: Designs vary, so archeologists can often tell the village it was made in and what period it came from.

the GREAT AMERICAN **BIRDWATCH**

TURKEY VULTURE
The Turkey Vulture is huge; Its wingspan can be up to six feet. It feeds almost exclusively on carrion, or dead animals.

ROCKY MOUNTAIN
NATIONAL PARK

With 100 mountain peaks more than 10,000 feet tall, the Rocky Mountains were certainly a hardship to cross for American pioneers heading west in the mid-1800s. Today, however, this national park offers an array of delights for the sports-minded. You can simply take in the breathtaking views or go extreme: camping, hiking, rock climbing and mountaineering, fishing, snowshoeing, and skiing are everywhere. And on Longs Peak, perhaps the most famous area of the park, you can spy thousands of climbers every year.

If you're an animal lover, no matter where you are in the park—tundras, high elevations, down by the lakes and streams—there's plenty to see. Elk, bears, moose, cougars, bighorn sheep, and hundreds of smaller animals are all on parade for your viewing—and sometimes frighteningly close!

RANGER FACT

Running through the park is the Great Continental Divide. All precipitation falls to one side of these mountains or the other, and eventually feeds into the Atlantic or the Pacific.

ROCKY MOUNTAIN NATIONAL PARK 1939

CLIMB FAMED LONGS PEAK · 14,255 ft
GUIDED ASCENTS AVAILABLE

from BOULDERFIELD SHELTER CABIN
LEAVING DAILY AT 6:50 AM AND 10:50 AM
$1.50 PER PERSON

· NO MODERN CONVENIENCES
· NO TREES TO SPOIL VIEW
· GUESTS ARRIVE ON FOOT OR HORSEBACK (NO AUTOS)
· FREEZING TEMPERATURES GUARANTEED OUTDOORS EVERY NIGHT
· WATER CARRIED FROM SNOWBANKS A FEW FEET FROM DOOR

ROCKY MOUNTAIN NATIONAL PARK
U.S. DEPARTMENT OF THE INTERIOR
NATIONAL PARK SERVICE

By the Numbers

1915: Year park was established

265,770: Acres in the park

359: Miles of trails

150: Lakes

450: Miles of streams

14,259: Height (in feet) of Longs Peak, the park's highest elevation

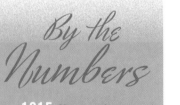

the GREAT AMERICAN BIRDWATCH

BROAD-TAILED HUMMINGBIRD

It's not the smallest hummingbird, but its iridescent green back and bright red throat may make the Broad-Tailed Hummingbird the most beautiful. Though it is not a songbird, the male's wings move so fast that they make a trilling sound while flying.

By the Numbers

1990: Year park was established

37: Original number of acres on the farm

110: Acres on the farm today

100 +: People who have been artists-in-residence at the farm

WEIR FARM
NATIONAL HISTORIC SITE

Though Weir Farm has more than one hundred beautiful, pastoral acres, neither the geography nor the topography accounts for this park's designation as a national historic site. The former home of J. Alden Weir (1852–1919), a famous American impressionist painter, is an artists' colony and the only national park dedicated to American painting.

In 1882, Weir came here from his home in New York City. He stayed to paint the surrounding landscapes, some of which still look the same as they do in his paintings. Other painters began to visit and stayed to paint, and when Weir died, his daughter took over the farm. Artists from all over the world have come here ever since, to get away from the hustle and bustle of daily life, to find comfort in the landscape, and to concentrate on creating their art. Visitors can tour Weir's original studio, walk through the same New England countryside he loved, and even go biking on a short trail.

The butterflies love the plants and flowers here at Weir Farm, and, in 2009, an annual butterfly walk and count began. So far, a dozen different species have been spotted, from the relatively common monarch to rarer specimens like the great spangled fritillary, the summer azure, and the question mark. There are also lots of frogs and salamanders, which you might see on your trail hike.

Have you ever wondered what it would be like to be an artist yourself, even though you're still a kid, and not yet a famous painter? Good news: There are summer Art Explorer classes offered right here on the farm.

AMAZING BUT TRUE!

On summer visits, you may be offered pastels, watercolors, graphite or colored pencils, and paper to take on your tour. You can have your own artistic experience—and take home the results!

RANGER FACT

Impressionism is a school of art, which began in mid-nineteenth century Paris, in which artists paint an impression of a landscape, instead of attempting to make their work more realistic. Impressionism changed the way artists did their work: It was the first time they actually left the studio and went outside to paint!

THE OTHER
NATIONAL PARK
In
CONNECTICUT

Quinebaug & Shetucket Rivers Valley
NATIONAL HERITAGE CORRIDOR

the
GREAT AMERICAN
BIRDWATCH

TURKEY

You might easily spot a turkey here: They are the largest of the birds that live in forests. Most of the species cannot fly because their weight makes them too heavy to get airborne. A group of turkeys are often called a gobble, or a rafter.

By the Numbers

1937: Year refuge was established

25: Square miles in the park

8: Miles along the Delaware River in the park

1: Dollar price of a duck stamp in 1934

15: Dollar price of a duck stamp today

BOMBAY HOOK
NATIONAL WILDLIFE REFUGE

A rest area would never be called a national park, would it? Well, in this case it is, because Bombay Hook National Wildlife Refuge is a rest area for birds.

Have you ever thought about how birds manage to make those long journeys flying south each winter? How do they eat? Where do they stop for a break? Bombay Hook, which has been protected land and a refuge and breeding ground since 1937, is one such spot. Birds tend to use a route to their destination that has few obstacles, like mountains, and plenty of food and water; on America's East Coast they travel from Canada to Mexico along what's called the Atlantic Flyway. The hundreds of thousands of birds that come to Bombay Hook every year find marsh grass, water, fish, other foods, and a sheltering landscape before they move on, including salt and freshwater pools, swampland, forests and fields. For humans, there's a twelve-mile car route, five nature trails, and three observation towers—you'll find more than 250 species of birds here to capture with cameras and view through binoculars.

And here's an ironic fact: Most of the money to save this refuge came from the Migratory Bird Hunting Stamp Act. Usually just called the Duck Stamp Act, it's the revenue the government collects from hunters every year for a license.

the GREAT AMERICAN BIRDWATCH

BALD EAGLE
All during the fall months, hundreds of thousands of birds stop here as they migrate. But Bald Eagles can be seen here most of the year; their eggs are laid in February, and after most birds are gone, you can still see eagles perched on empty branches in December.

AMAZING *BUT TRUE!*

An Indian chief sold this refuge area in 1679 for one gun, four handfuls of gunpowder, three waistcoats, one flask of liquor, and one kettle!

MIGRATORY BIRD HUNTING STAMP
U.S. DEPARTMENT OF AGRICULTURE
VOID AFTER JUNE 30, 1937.
$1

THE OTHER
NATIONAL PARK In
DELAWARE

Captain John Smith Chesapeake
NATIONAL HISTORIC TRAIL

By the Numbers

1988: Year site established

9: Acres in the park

14: Rooms in the original home

21: Rooms in Cedar Hill at Douglass's death

1: Rooms in the "Growlery," the retreat on the site where Douglass worked and wrote

FREDERICK DOUGLASS
NATIONAL HISTORIC SITE

You might have thought that a historic site in our nation's capital would have something to do with a former president or the government. But Frederick Douglass was certainly one of the most important Americans to shape our country's history.

RANGER FACT

Frederick Douglass did a lot of work with the Underground Railroad, the name given to the various secret routes slaves took from the South to escape to freedom.

AMAZING BUT TRUE!

Frederick Douglass was also an early suffragist, believing in equal rights, including the right to vote, for women.

Douglass was born a slave, and after several attempts as a young man, escaped and became an abolitionist, dedicating his life to ending slavery. He ranks among the most prominent civil rights activists in history; he was also a statesman and an author. Douglass lived here, at Cedar Hill, from 1877 to 1895, years after slavery had ended and during a period when the nation was still recovering from the devastation of the Civil War.

"I will unite with anybody to do right and with no one to do wrong."
—FREDERICK DOUGLASS

OTHER NATIONAL PARKS In DISTRICT OF COLUMBIA

African American Civil War MEMORIAL
Anacostia PARK
Battlegound NATIONAL CEMETERY
Capitol Hill PARKS
Chesapeake & Ohio Canal NATIONAL HISTORICAL PARK
Chesapeake Bay GATEWAYS NETWORK
Constitution Gardens
Ford's Theatre NATIONAL HISTORIC SITE
Fort Dupont PARK
Franklin Delano Roosevelt MEMORIAL
Frederick Douglass NATIONAL HISTORIC SITE
George Mason MEMORIAL

George Washington MEMORIAL PARKWAY
John Ericsson NATIONAL MEMORIAL
Kenilworth PARK & AQUATIC GARDENS
Korean War Veterans MEMORIAL
Lincoln MEMORIAL
Mary McLeod Bethune Council House NATIONAL HISTORIC SITE
National Capital Parks-East NATIONAL MALL
National Mall & Memorial PARKS
National World War II MEMORIAL
Old Post Office Tower
The Old Stone House
Peirce Mill
Pennsylvania Avenue NATIONAL HISTORIC SITE
Potomac Heritage NATIONAL SCENIC TRAIL
President's Park (THE WHITE HOUSE)
Rock Creek Park
Sewall-Belmont House NATIONAL HISTORIC SITE
Thomas Jefferson MEMORIAL
Vietnam Veterans MEMORIAL
Washington MONUMENT

By the Numbers

1947: Year park was established

1,508,571: Acres in the park

50+: Kinds of reptiles living in the park

102°F: Highest recorded temperature, in 1996

24°F: Lowest recorded temperature, in 1977

6 million: People in Florida who get their drinking water from the Everglades

RANGER FACT

Airboats, which are propelled by gigantic fans, are used in the Everglades because the vegetation and shallow waters would ruin a submerged propeller.

EVERGLADES
NATIONAL PARK

the GREAT AMERICAN BIRDWATCH

WHITE IBIS

It's no surprise that wading birds are common in the Everglades: There are sixteen different species of them here. The most common is the White Ibis, the long, slender bird that lives almost exclusively on crayfish. It is a sociable bird, which feeds and nests in large flocks.

The third-largest park in the continental United States, the Everglades is the most unusual environmentally. It is a world like no other, and seems almost prehistoric in places, even though it has only been around for five thousand years. And it's not an endless marsh, as so many people think: It's actually a very slow river, moving about a quarter-mile a day, starting at Lake Okeechobee, and emptying into Florida Bay.

But most people think of wildlife when you think of the Everglades, and it's full of incredible animals: snakes, turtles, panthers, manatees, and more. There are birds that swim, fish that breathe air, cacti that live in water, and plants that eat meat. It is also the only place in the world where alligators and crocodiles live side by side. But cover up: The one thing the Everglades has more of than anything else is insects. The mosquitoes are so vicious, they've been known to bite alligators!

AMAZING BUT TRUE!

Before the Everglades became a national park in 1947, "Gladesmen" lived here, fishing, hunting, and generally surviving off the land.

CASTILLO DE
SAN MARCOS
NATIONAL MONUMENT

By the Numbers

1924: Year park was established

2½: Acres comprising the fort itself

320: Acres in the park

205: Years of service for the fort

23: Years it took to build the fort (1672–1695)

RANGER FACT

Although five different countries have had control of the fort during its history, it has never once been taken by force.

Originally known as Castillo de San Marcos (Castle of Saint Mark), and later known as Fort Marion, the oldest masonry fort in the United States has withstood 330 years of bombardment and hurricanes. During its long history, flags from six different countries flew over its battle-scarred walls. The fact that it is still standing is due to the unusual stone with which is was built. It's known as *coquina*, which is Spanish for "small shell," and that's exactly what it is—a form of limestone naturally made from tiny shells. When the fort was under attack, cannonballs would sink into its soft walls, rather than destroying them.

The fort has protected people in several wars. In 1702, every resident of Saint Augustine and the soldiers fighting the attacking British were kept safe behind its walls for two entire months. Since 1875, it was mainly used as a military prison, housing Native Americans during the Indian Wars to 1898, when Spanish-American War deserters were kept here.

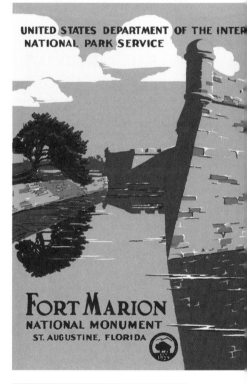

UNITED STATES DEPARTMENT OF THE INTER... NATIONAL PARK SERVICE

FORT MARION
NATIONAL MONUMENT
ST. AUGUSTINE, FLORIDA

the GREAT AMERICAN BIRDWATCH

PELICAN

The Pelican is seen throughout Florida. Pelicans dive for fish and hold them in their pouchlike throat. Pelicans can bend their heads back to rub their heads on glands near their tail feathers—there they get oil to rub all over their bodies to weatherproof themselves!

AMAZING BUT TRUE!

There is a room in the fort shut off by the park rangers that is thought to be haunted by the ghosts of prisoners who died there. TV's *Ghost Adventures* came to investigate!

OTHER NATIONAL PARKS In FLORIDA

Big Cypress NATIONAL PRESERVE
Biscayne NATIONAL PARK
Canaveral NATIONAL SEASHORE
De Soto NATIONAL MEMORIAL
Dry Tortugas NATIONAL PARK
Fort Caroline NATIONAL MEMORIAL
Fort Matanzas NATIONAL MONUMENT
Gulf Islands NATIONAL SEASHORE
Timucuan ECOLOGICAL & HISTORIC PRESERVE

By the Numbers

1971: Year park was established

18 x 3: Size of the island, in miles

2: Gallons of seashells, shark teeth, sea stars, sea urchins, and sand dollars a person can collect during a visit

80: Percentage of the island owned by the National Park Service

1: Number of camping sites on the island

0: Number of stores on the island

100: Eggs laid by the island's loggerhead turtles in each nest

333: Species of birds recorded on the island

CUMBERLAND ISLAND
NATIONAL SEASHORE

CUMBERLAND
ISLAND
NATIONAL SEASHORE

Cumberland Island, off the southern shores of Georgia, is one of the most unspoiled places in the country, with very few residents. But it does have an illustrious, storied history.

As long as four thousand years ago, the Timucua Indians lived on the island. After the American Revolution, war hero General Nathaniel Greene joined forces with the inventor of the cotton gin, Eli Whitney, and started cotton plantations here. It later became a retreat for some of America's wealthy, most notably Thomas Carnegie, brother of industrialist Andrew Carnegie, and his family. They gradually bought 90 percent of the island and built a mansion named Dungeness in 1886. Dungeness burned to the ground in 1959 and soon after the Carnegies sold the island to the federal government. Visitors can now tour the mansion's ruins.

However, most visitors come to see the beaches and wildlife. The most beautiful are the wild horses, but you can also spot sea turtles, wild hogs, armadillos, and abundant shorebirds. The largest population of sharks on the East Coast surround Cumberland Island. Off the northern tip of the island is a depression in the seafloor, known as the "Eighty Foot Hole," which is home to the largest sharks in the Atlantic Ocean.

AMAZING
BUT TRUE!

Oak trees from Cumberland Island were used to build the USS *Constitution*, the oldest ship in the navy, which was launched in 1797.

the
GREAT AMERICAN
BIRDWATCH

AMERICAN OYSTERCATCHER
The American Oystercatcher is a shorebird with a long, heavy, red beak. Its beak is so strong the Oystercatcher can open shellfish like oysters, clams, and mussels. A cousin of the American Oystercatcher, the Black Oystercatcher, is found on parts of the Pacific Coast.

OTHER
NATIONAL PARKS
|||||||||| In ||||||||||
GEORGIA

Andersonville
NATIONAL HISTORIC SITE
Chattahoochee River
NATIONAL RECREATION AREA
Chickamauga & Chattanooga
NATIONAL MILITARY PARK
Fort Frederica
NATIONAL MONUMENT
Fort Pulaski NATIONAL MONUMENT
Jimmy Carter
NATIONAL HISTORIC SITE
Martin Luther King Jr.
NATIONAL HISTORIC SITE
Ocmulgee NATIONAL MONUMENT

RANGER
FACT

While beautiful shells are easy to find, it is more fun to look for the shark teeth found along the shores.

the GREAT AMERICAN BIRDWATCH

GUAM RAIL

The Guam Rail, or Ko'Ko became flightless several thousand years ago because of a lack of predators. Now the Ko'Ko has become easy prey for the brown tree snake. Nearly extinct, some of these flightless birds are being raised in captivity, in hopes of increasing the population.

WAR IN THE PACIFIC
NATIONAL HISTORIC PARK

Guam, a U.S. territory in the Pacific Ocean, was an ideal target for Japan in World War II. So the Japanese began to bomb Guam, where there were American military bases, only hours after they bombed Pearl Harbor in Hawaii. The Pearl Harbor attack prompted our country's entrance into the war. The Japanese held Guam from 1941 to 1944.

RANGER FACT

Tourism is Guam's primary business: *Hafa Adai!* is the friendly way residents greet you. This phrase means "Hello" or "How are you" in Chamarro, the native language of the islanders.

And that's what makes this park different: It is the only one in the national parks system dedicated to the men and women who fought in the Pacific during World War II. Parts of the park are spread all over the island: You can visit guns, trenches, caves, and battlefields. Then, get your snorkeling gear and dive in—there are over two hundred kinds of coral in the surrounding waters.

By the Numbers

1978: Year park was established

13: Degrees north, in latitude, Guam is from the equator

2,037: Acres in the park

16,142: Names of war casualties on the memorial wall

3,500+: Marine species in nearby waters

AMAZING BUT TRUE!

A brown tree snake that snuck onto an arriving ship has killed off much of Guam's bird population. Though not fatal to humans, its offspring have eaten most of the birds.

HAWAII

MEET THE **INTERPRETIVE PARK NATURALIST**
AT **KILAUEA SUMMIT**

for ALL DAY HIKES TO
SULPHUR BANKS
STEAM VENTS
FERN JUNGLE
LAVA TUBE

HALEMAUMAU -
HOME OF THE
FIRE GODDESS PELE

HAWAII
NATIONAL PARK
U.S. DEPARTMENT NATIONAL PARK
OF THE INTERIOR SERVICE

EST
1916

HAWAII

VOLCANOES
NATIONAL PARK

Most people visit this park to see two of the world's most active volcanoes, Kilauea and Mauna Loa, and the various vents and tunnels that spew forth a fiery show of lava. But that's not all there is to see. This huge national park on the island of Hawaii also has a bleak desert formed from volcanic ash that destroyed all the plants. And there's a lush rain forest you can explore. In a single trip, you can go from sea level all the way to the top of Mauna Loa, the world's largest volcano, which covers half the island of Hawaii.

By the Numbers

1916: Year park was established

505.36: Square miles in the park

13,677: Height, in feet, of Mauna Loa volcano, which is 2,000 feet taller than Mount Everest

400: Mauna Loa's circumference, in miles

2,150°F: The measured temperature of molten lava at Mauna Loa

568: Acres of new land added by the lava erupting from Kilauea since 1983

700,000 to **1** million: How long ago, in years, Mauna Loa began erupting

OTHER
NATIONAL PARKS
|||||||||| In ||||||||||
HAWAII

Ala Kahakai
NATIONAL HISTORIC TRAIL
Haleakala NATIONAL PARK
Kalaupapa
NATIONAL HISTORICAL PARK
Kaloko-Honokohau
NATIONAL HISTORICAL PARK
Pu'ukohola Heiau
NATIONAL HISTORIC SITE
Pu'uhonua O Honaunau
NATIONAL HISTORICAL PARK
USS Arizona MEMORIAL
World War II Valor in the Pacific
NATIONAL MONUMENT

AMAZING BUT TRUE!
Though the word *vulcanism* sounds like it may have something to do with *Star Trek*, it actually means the study of volcanic activity.

RANGER FACT
The Volcano House is the only hotel in the park; it was first built in 1846—as a grass shack.

Hundreds of years ago, the native Hawaiians believed that the other famous volcano here, Kilauea, was the home of a goddess named Pele, and they would travel here to offer gifts and prayers to her, never knowing if the massive crater would explode with lava. In fact, you can see footprints here, thought to be left by women and children as they ran from the erupting Kilauea in 1790; many were killed in that disaster. There are still frequent eruptions, and parts of the park have to be closed for long periods; occasionally, when the lava has cooled, roads and fields may have risen well over fifty feet.

Take some time to go camping and hiking here, if you can: The park is an International Biosphere Reserve and World Heritage Site, and it's crisscrossed by lots of hiking trails. Some take you close to slow-moving lava. But if you only have a few hours, take the eleven-mile drive to the top of Kilauea: You'll be able to see the desert and rain forests on that trip. And don't miss the Jaggar Museum, where you can see cool volcano-tracking equipment like seismographs.

the
GREAT AMERICAN
BIRDWATCH

HAWAIIAN GOOSE
The Hawaiian state bird is the Hawaiian Goose, sometimes called the Nene because of the sound it makes. You'll notice a resemblance to the smaller Canada Goose, probably its ancestor about half a million years ago. Now it is the world's rarest species: It only lives on a few of Hawaii's islands.

FRANK CHURCH
RIVER OF NO RETURN
WILDERNESS

The River of No Return. **Sounds scary, doesn't it? Its real name is actually the Salmon River, but the current is so strong that people say you can't make your way back trying to paddle upstream. However, if you like white-water rafting, you're in for a great ride!**

Who's Frank Church? He was a U.S. senator from Idaho who helped pass the Wilderness Act of 1964. This is the second largest wilderness area in the continental United States, right after Death Valley. His name was added shortly before his death in 1984.

The Salmon River flows deep down in a canyon, like the Grand Canyon, but here, instead of looking up at steep, rocky walls, you'll see beautiful forest. Some 1.5 million acres make up this wilderness, with nearly three hundred trails covering over 2,600 miles. And perhaps even more exciting is the wildlife: Coyotes, mountain lions, gray wolves, moose, elk, wolverines, lynx, mountain goats, and black and grizzly bears all can be found here. For fun, there are jet boats and horse-packing trips, rafting, fishing, and hiking on trails from easy to difficult. This is America at its most beautiful.

RANGER FACT

Jet boats are allowed here in this natural setting because they were "grandfathered" in—meaning, they were already in use and therefore permitted—before the Wilderness Act went into effect.

AMAZING BUT TRUE!

"The Frank," as it is called, is separated from the adjoining wilderness area, the Selway-Bitterroot, by nothing but a dirt road.

the GREAT AMERICAN BIRDWATCH

MOUNTAIN BLUEBIRD

The Mountain Bluebird is Idaho's state bird, though it might seem a misnomer when you spy the female, who is quite gray. The male, however, is a brilliant blue. These birds like to nest in a hollow and have had help from lots of human friends who have built nest boxes for them.

OTHER NATIONAL PARKS In IDAHO

California NATIONAL HISTORIC TRAIL
City of Rocks NATIONAL RESERVE
Craters of the Moon NATIONAL MONUMENT & PRESERVE
Hagerman Fossil Beds NATIONAL MONUMENT
Lewis & Clark NATIONAL HISTORIC TRAIL
Minidoka Internment NATIONAL MONUMENT
Nez Perce NATIONAL HISTORIC TRAIL
Nez Perce NATIONAL HISTORICAL PARK
Oregon NATIONAL HISTORIC TRAIL
Yellowstone NATIONAL PARK

1980: Year park was established

2,366,827: Acres in the park

8: Species of big game animals in the wilderness

10: Inches of rainfall annually in the Salmon River

114: Number of bridges on the trails in the wilderness

" A wilderness, in contrast with those areas where man and his own works dominate the landscape, is hereby recognized as an area where the earth and community of life are untrammeled by man, where man himself is a visitor who does not remain."

—FROM THE 1964 WILDERNESS ACT

1933: Year park was established

265,616: Acres in the park

9: Number of Illinois counties the park spans

4: Number of feet wide the 1,000-mile trail system in the park is

146: Miles of rivers and streams in the forest

200+: Lakes and ponds in the forest

SHAWNEE
NATIONAL FOREST

Hundreds of millions of years ago, the Laurentide ice sheet covered most of the state of Illinois. A part of the land where the glacier receded is now the Shawnee National Forest, creating such wonders as the Little Grand Canyon, a gulch that drops nearly two hundred feet into the Big Muddy River.

Beyond the glacier, we have the Civilian Conservation Corps to thank for lots of the beauty in the forest. In the beginning of the twentieth century, much of this territory was worn-out farmland. But then the corps, made up of workers paid by the government during the Great Depression, planted numerous pine trees to enrich the soil. The corps also created six lakes, including Roosevelt Lake.

However, they did not have a hand in creating the Garden of the Gods, a combination of beautiful old trees, cliffs, and strange and wonderful rock formations. The bedrock of this area, which was created more than 320 million years ago, extends into the earth more than four miles deep! Some of the more popular rock formations surrounding the sandstone cliffs are Camel Rock, Mushroom Rock, and Anvil Rock.

And don't miss the hiking, horseback riding, rock climbing, and fishing that's here to enjoy. More than 500 wildlife species can be found within the forest, including 48 mammals, 237 birds, 52 reptiles, 57 amphibians, and 109 species of fish. You can even stay in a real log cabin!

RANGER FACT

Careful: Part of the Shawnee is closed off every year so poisonous snakes like the copperhead, cottonmouth, and timber rattlers can migrate. No one wants you or the snakes to get hurt!

AMAZING BUT TRUE!

Ten percent of the forest is made up of seven wilderness areas. In these areas, you can only travel by foot or on horseback.

OTHER
NATIONAL PARKS
IIIIIIIIIIII In IIIIIIIIIIIII
ILLINOIS

Illinois & Michigan Canal
NATIONAL HERITAGE CENTER
Lincoln Home
NATIONAL HISTORIC SITE

BLACK-NECKED STILT

Much of Shawnee is wetlands, and for this reason the Black-Necked Stilt fits right in, though you'll usually find it along a coastline in the rest of the country. It's no surprise that stilt is part of its name: Look at its long, skinny legs! And its pointed black bill is good for hunting and capturing tiny insects and their eggs in the mud and sand.

The
GREAT AMERICAN
BIRDWATCH

AMAZING BUT TRUE!

Founded in 1732, Vincennes is the oldest community in Indiana inhabited by Europeans or Americans.

the GREAT AMERICAN BIRDWATCH

the
GREAT AMERICAN
BIRDWATCH

CARDINAL

The Cardinal, or Redbird, is the state bird of Indiana and six other states: Illinois, Ohio, North Carolina, Kentucky, Virginia, and West Virginia. The male of this abundant American bird is bright red with pointed plumage on its head; the female is much browner, with a little red on the chest.

GEORGE ROGERS
CLARK
NATIONAL HISTORICAL PARK

Have you heard of William Clark of the famed Lewis and Clark Expedition? This park is dedicated to his older brother, the brave Lieutenant George Rogers Clark, a hero of the American Revolution. Clark led his troops eighteen days through cold temperatures and freezing water, often as high as their necks, to get to Fort Sackville in the city of Vincennes. When he captured Fort Sackville from the British, he won with it control of an immense area of land that would eventually become our states of Illinois, Indiana, Michigan, Ohio, and Wisconsin.

In the 1920s, plans were made to memorialize Clark, his men's bravery, and America's spirit and fortitude by building the George Rogers Clark Memorial here on the banks of the Wabash River. Visitors can go inside this grand rotunda and see murals depicting Clark's epic struggles and success; there is also a movie of Clark's campaign.

By the Numbers

1931: Year park was established

24.3: Acres in the park

16 x 28: Size, in feet, of the 7 murals in the rotunda

7.2: City of Vincennes' area, in square miles

6: Number of weeks old the rotunda was before it started leaking!

27: Clark's age when he took back Fort Sackville

OTHER
NATIONAL PARKS
In
INDIANA

Indiana Dunes
NATIONAL LAKESHORE

Lincoln Boyhood
NATIONAL MEMORIAL

RANGER FACT

Ezra Winter, who painted the murals in the Clark Rotunda, also painted several others at Washington, D.C.'s Library of Congress and Rockefeller Center in New York City.

AMAZING *BUT TRUE!*

When European settlers came here and found rich, fertile soil, they plowed under many effigy mounds so they could plant crops.

Your first questions about these giant mounds of dirt are no doubt going to be, "What are these?" and "Why did building them end as suddenly as it began?" The second question may always remain a mystery, but the first can certainly be answered, at least in part.

EFFIGY MOUNDS
NATIONAL MONUMENT

Effigy mounds are raised piles of dirt, first formed, archeologists say, by the Indians of the Woodlands period around 500 BC. We think they were primarily built for religious purposes and were considered sacred sites—many Native Americans still feel that way. They also believe in the power of animal spirits, so as you walk through the effigy mounds you'll see the familiar shapes of birds, bears, deer, snakes, turtles, and more. There are also linear and conically shaped mounds, probably used as burial sites; they might have divided hunting areas and territories, too. They are certainly mysterious, and very beautiful.

There are no cars allowed here, but you can walk among the mounds for a few hours, or hike for days: the South Unit has 29 mounds, the North Unit, 67. Eleven miles away is the third unit, called Sny McGill, with 112 mounds. Stop first at the visitors' center and see a short film about the Moundbuilders, then explore this mystical, magical national park.

RANGER FACT

Native Americans built the most effigy mounds in what is now the state of Wisconsin—perhaps up to twenty thousand, about four thousand of which remain today.

the GREAT AMERICAN BIRDWATCH
EASTERN GOLDFINCH

The Eastern Goldfinch, Iowa's state bird, is also known as the wild canary. The female is more brown than gold, but the male is bright yellow with a black cap, wings, and tail. This little bird tends to stay put through the cold Iowa winters, living on seeds of dandelions ragweed and evening primrose. It often lives among the sunflowers, where it finds plenty more seeds to eat.

THE OTHER
NATIONAL PARK
||||||||||| *In* |||||||||||
IOWA
Herbert Hoover
NATIONAL HISTORIC SITE

By the Numbers

1949: Year park was established

2,526.39: Acres in the park

14: Miles of hiking trails in the park

31: Number of mounds that are shaped like animals

88,000+: Visitors annually to the park

▷ **BIRD'S-EYE-VIEW**
One of the largest effigies is the Great Bear Mound, which is 137 feet long and 70 feet wide.

▷ A NEW KIND OF PARK

The National Park Service has joined hands with the Nature Conservancy to help manage Tallgrass Prairie. The conservancy works in every state and many countries around the world to preserve the animals, plants, and natural habitats that represent the diversity of life on this planet by protecting its lands and waters.

TALLGRASS PRAIRIE
NATIONAL PRESERVE

In the Flint Hills of Kansas, you'll find prairie as far as the eye can see. And though it may seem endless, it's almost all that's left in America of the tallgrass prairie. Eighty percent of the prairie is made up of forty to sixty different grasses. Less than fifty years ago, there were more than 400,000 square miles of prairie. Since then, all but 4 percent has been plowed under to make way for cities, shopping malls, roads, and various other kinds of development. The prairie and its ecosystem are an integral part of disappearing American life and history, the result of long-ago glaciers that made this land flat.

Part of this park was a ranch in the 1870s; you can visit the ranch house, and a huge stone barn, where there are artifacts and a short film. Then, hike or take a seven-mile bus tour that stops at the highest point here, where you can see the grasslands of the Flint Hills rolling away from you like waves in the ocean. And if you think you spot something loping along in the distance, your eyes may not be deceiving you. A small herd of bison, also known as American buffalo, were returned to the prairie by the Nature Conservancy. In 2010, the first bison was born here in nearly 150 years.

AMAZING BUT TRUE!

Collared lizards, which live at the preserve, can run on their hind legs with a stride that reaches more than three times the length of their bodies.

RANGER FACT

Sixty million bison once roamed the plains in the early days of our country; by the early 1900s they had been hunted to near extinction.

OTHER NATIONAL PARKS In KANSAS

Brown v. Board of Education
NATIONAL HISTORIC SITE

Fort Larned
NATIONAL HISTORIC SITE

Fort Scott NATIONAL HISTORIC SITE

Nicodemus
NATIONAL HISTORIC SITE

the GREAT AMERICAN BIRDWATCH

PRAIRIE CHICKENS

Yes, there really is a bird called the Prairie Chicken! These medium-sized relatives of the Grouse, are quite plump. They feast on seeds, fruit, and insects in the Kansas tallgrass. Their numbers have fallen dramatically elsewhere, however, and efforts are being made to repopulate other regions by moving them.

CUMBERLAND
GAP
NATIONAL HISTORICAL PARK

Carved by wind and water, Cumberland Gap is a natural break in the Appalachian Mountain chain. Native Americans used this break for centuries to travel easily from east to west through the mountains. One of our country's great frontiersmen, Daniel Boone, was hired in 1775 to create the Wilderness Road for pioneers to cross the gap. Over the next thirty-five years, approximately 300,000 people used the gap to settle in Kentucky, which was then complete wilderness.

Stretching twenty-six miles along the Cumberland Mountain, the park boasts two can't-miss attractions: the Hensley Settlement and Gap Cave. At the beginning of the twentieth century, two families moved to Brush Mountain to live a self-sufficient, pioneer lifestyle. Their experiment only lasted about fifty years, but the Hensley Settlement remains. You can stroll through and see the blacksmith's shop, a one-room schoolhouse, and rustic cabins—all Internet-free!

The Gap Cave is one of twenty-four limestone caves in the park. It's sixteen miles long, and there are two-hour tours where you'll see huge stalagmites, cascades, and bats! Historians think soldiers from both sides of the Civil War may have used the cave for storage of ammunition and other supplies, and as a hospital.

Then, before leaving, take a hike up to Pinnacle Overlook for the view—you might even see an elk, black bear, opossum, or wild turkey on the way.

AMAZING BUT TRUE!

Buffalo were migrating through the Cumberland Gap long before humans discovered it.

The GREAT AMERICAN BIRDWATCH
RED-TAILED HAWK

The Red-Tailed Hawk is commonly found in these parts. The female is larger than the male, and their long, easy glide overhead, searching for prey, is a familiar sight. They are also easily trained, so they're a popular choice for falconry.

OTHER NATIONAL PARKS In KENTUCKY

Abraham Lincoln Birthplace
NATIONAL HISTORICAL PARK
Mammoth Cave NATIONAL PARK

KISATCHIE
NATIONAL FOREST

Named after an Indian tribe, Kisatchie is the only national forest in all of Louisiana. It's filled with pine and hardwood and eerie bayou. This is a very unusual sort of park; for one thing, it's not just one land area. Rather, it's divided up into six separate sections around the middle of the state. Nor is it dedicated to any historic landmark or historic occurrence, but just to its beautiful natural surroundings.

RANGER FACT

Kisatchie seems to have everything—even the Catahoula Hummingbird and Butterfly Garden, an acre of special plants and flowers that attracts plenty of both species. It's a little like walking through a fairy tale!

OTHER NATIONAL PARKS In LOUISIANA

Cane River Creole
NATIONAL HISTORICAL PARK
Jean Lafitte
NATIONAL HISTORIC PARK & PRESERVE
New Orleans Jazz
NATIONAL HISTORICAL PARK
Poverty Point
NATIONAL MONUMENT

And Kisatchie is full of fun: The forest sports over forty different recreation areas. There are more than 100 miles of hiking trails; you can also picnic, hunt, swim, fish, ride a horse or a mountain bike, and camp anywhere you want. Make sure to check out the thirteen-mile water trail in the Saline Bayou, which you can float down in a boat or a canoe. Wildlife abounds in the forest: Be prepared to spot coyotes, foxes, Louisiana black bears, otters, bobcats, snakes—even wild boars and herds of wild horses.

We owe the existence of this park to a woman named Carolyn Dorman. A collector of trees and shrubs, she was also the first woman ever to work for the U.S. Forest Service. She started working there in 1921. Next thing anyone knew, she had persuaded the Louisiana legislature, the Forest Service, and Congress to establish Kisatchie National Forest. There is even a Carolyn Dorman Nature Preserve. This shows the power of just one person who wants to make a difference.

AMAZING BUT TRUE!

A high school student, Kevin Allen, began a search at Kisatchie for a rare orchid called the Kentucky ladyslipper, in order to make sure it did not become extinct. It took him three years to find the orchid in flower!

the GREAT AMERICAN BIRDWATCH

REDHEADED WOODPECKER

Though easier to spot elsewhere in the country, the cockaded Redheaded Woodpecker has become a rare sighting in Louisiana. Conservationists have tried to lure these woodpeckers by building artificial cavities in long-leaf pines, hoping they'll come there to nest.

By the Numbers

1930: Year the park was designated as a national forest

604,000: Acres in the forest

7: Parishes (counties) in Louisiana the park spans

300: Height, in feet, of Carolyn Dorman's favorite tree, a long-leaf pine she called "Grandpappy"

15: Millions of dollars the United States paid for the Louisiana Territory in 1803 (the so-called Louisiana Purchase, negotiated by President Thomas Jefferson)

100+: Miles of hiking trails in the forest

ACADIA
NATIONAL PARK

By the Numbers

1916: Year the park was established

47,390: Acres in the park

2,225,000+: Visitors annually to the park

120+: Miles of hiking trails

45: Miles of carriage trails for walking or biking

1,528: Height, in feet, of Cadillac Mountain

Acadia is a national park made of islands, the largest of which is Mount Desert Island, the third-largest island on the East Coast. This is Maine at its best: beautiful, sometimes quiet and empty, with craggy beaches and cold, cold water—only about 55 degrees Fahrenheit, even in the height of summer! But there's a lot to do here, both on land and on the water.

RANGER FACT

Though many people come here for a short hike or a drive, the average stay at Acadia is three to four days.

ACADIA NATIONAL PARK 1939

In Acadia, you'll find mountains, shoreline, lakes, and plenty of woodland: You can hike, camp, ride bikes, and even take a ride in a horse-drawn carriage. Wealthy industrialist John D. Rockefeller Jr., whose family had a summer home here on Mount Desert, designed and built carriage trails through the park, hoping to keep automobiles off the island. He didn't win that fight, but the carriages ride on.

Lots of folks like to start the day atop Cadillac Mountain—the tallest on the eastern coastline—to see the sunrise. The summit is so far east that in fall and winter, you'll be one of the first to see the rays of sun in the entire United States. Then, how about a Dive-in Theater Boat Cruise through Frenchman Bay? You can watch real-time video of a diver underwater as he finds cool marine life to bring back onboard for you to touch and explore!

Wildflowers are plentiful here in Acadia, too—colorful fields filled with beauties like bunchberries, bluebeard lilies, asters, violets, goldenrod, and the rare twinflower, which has two stems, each with a single bloom at the top. But don't leave without seeing the shell mounds. They're actually a gigantic dump heap for shellfish remains, started thousands of years ago by the Indians who fished and lived nearby. Some have been found that were up to thirty feet high!

the GREAT AMERICAN BIRDWATCH

OSPREY

The Osprey is a raptor, but this one prefers fish; Ospreys swoop down and capture them in their talons. Ospreys will build a nest very near to a body of water, even if it's in a city; they are found nearly all over the world.

OTHER NATIONAL PARKS In MAINE

Maine Acadian Culture
Roosevelt Campobello
INTERNATIONAL PARK
Saint Croix Island
INTERNATIONAL HISTORIC SITE

AMAZING BUT TRUE!

The jagged lines of granite stones that act as guardrails on the side of the road on Mount Desert Island have been nicknamed "Rockefeller's teeth."

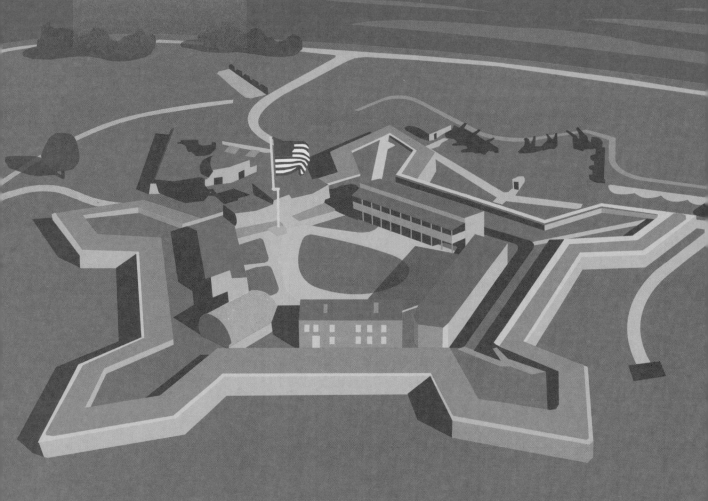

FORT McHENRY

NATIONAL MONUMENT AND HISTORIC SHRINE

Fort McHenry was built in 1798 at a time of peace, in order to be prepared to defend the country against any future enemies. This star-shaped battlement, named after James McHenry, secretary of war under George Washington, would protect the valuable port of Baltimore.

But war did come to Fort McHenry—many times and in many ways. It was used as a military prison during the Civil War; a hospital during World War I; and a Coast Guard base, keeping watch on the sea once again, during World War II. Only one time, during the War of 1812, has the fort been under attack, but it has become one of the most famous nights in America's history.

On the night of September 13, 1814, an American lawyer named Francis Scott Key was aboard a British ship, negotiating the release of some war prisoners. This is the night Fort McHenry had been built for. As a guest aboard the enemy ship, Key watched, helpless, as the British bombarded the Americans. When morning broke, and he saw the American flag still flying over Fort McHenry, Key was inspired to write a poem that became our national anthem, "The Star-Spangled Banner."

Here at the fort you can see a replica of that flag, and tour the grounds, barracks, guardhouse and more. You'll see firsthand what our soldiers were up against in the War of 1812's Battle of Baltimore, one of the United States' greatest victories.

the GREAT AMERICAN BIRDWATCH
WIGEON
Though the Baltimore Oriole is Maryland's state bird, Fort McHenry is home to lots of seabirds, like Wigeons, green-faced ducks that feed on the grasses around them. They'll steal food from other birds, so they're often called "robber ducks."

RANGER FACT
The star shape is not unusual for a fort built at that time. Each point allows for views of some of the other points across from it, so soldiers on watch can keep an eye on each other.

AMAZING BUT TRUE!
When a new state is added and the flag is redesigned, it is first flown over Fort McHenry. Hawaii was the last state to be added, on August 21, 1959.

OTHER NATificonAL PARKS *In* MARYLAND

Antietam
NATIONAL BATTLEFIELD AND CEMETERY
Assateague Island
NATIONAL SEASHORE
Baltimore-Washington PARKWAY
Catoctin Mountain PARK
Chesapeake and Ohio Canal
NATIONAL HISTORICAL PARK
Fort Washington PARK
Glen Echo PARK
Greenbelt PARK
Hampton NATIONAL HISTORIC SITE
Piscataway PARK
Suitland PARKWAY
Thomas Stone
NATIONAL HISTORIC SITE

OH SAY, CAN YOU SEE?
Fort McHenry is one of very few spots in the United States allowed to fly the flag twenty-four hours a day. And there's one more place where the flag flies continuously—on the surface of the moon, where it was placed by the astronauts of *Apollo 11*.

This park, and the city of Lowell, Massachusetts itself, is somewhat of a tribute to the Industrial Revolution. Around 1800, several inventions, like the steam engine, began to change the way we made things. Suddenly it wasn't just craftspeople making things by hand anymore—there were mills.

The Lowell mills mainly manufactured cotton cloth. Young women, usually between the ages of fifteen and twenty-five, would come here, live in boardinghouses, and work in the mills, often up to twelve hours a day. They made very little money, and their room and board were taken out of their wages. The mill that employed them kept a very strict watch over them: If they got rowdy, or didn't go to church on Sunday, they could lose their jobs. After World War II, many of these textile mills were abandoned, but in this park you can see what it was like to work at the dawn of industrial technology.

You can go to different places all over the city and get a taste of the early days of manufacturing. There are over five miles of canals, and the water from them powered the mills and the machinery inside. You can even take a canal tour with a ranger. Then see exactly what working in this mill town was like: Stop first at the Boott Cotton Mills Museum, where you'll find exhibits and visit a weaving room. Then the Patrick J. Mogan Cultural Center exhibits will show you just how the mill girls lived, and what it was like to be an immigrant almost two hundred years ago.

the GREAT AMERICAN BIRDWATCH

CHICKADEE

The Black-Capped Chickadee is the Massachusetts state bird, so named for its familiar black head and throat. It's extremely common all over the state, and most birders would not be able to tell it apart from its southern counterpart, the Carolina Chickadee, except for its song. However, in the states between where both might be found, they tend to learn each other's songs—and then it's really hard to tell!

AMAZING BUT TRUE!

For $1.25 per week, a mill girl got a shared bedroom, three meals a day, and laundry service—but the house rules were very strict!

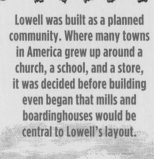

RANGER FACT

Lowell was built as a planned community. Where many towns in America grew up around a church, a school, and a store, it was decided before building even began that mills and boardinghouses would be central to Lowell's layout.

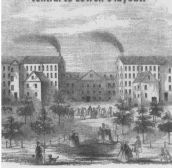

OTHER NATIONAL PARKS In MASSACHUSETTS

Adams NATIONAL HISTORICAL PARK
Boston African American NATIONAL HISTORICAL SITE
Boston Harbor Islands NATIONAL RECREATION AREA
Boston NATIONAL HISTORICAL PARK
Cape Cod NATIONAL SEASHORE
Frederick Law Olmsted NATIONAL HISTORIC SITE
John F. Kennedy NATIONAL HISTORIC SITE
Longfellow NATIONAL HISTORIC SITE
Minute Man NATIONAL HISTORICAL PARK
New Bedford Whaling NATIONAL HISTORICAL PARK
Salem Maritime NATIONAL HISTORIC SITE
Saugus Iron Works NATIONAL HISTORIC SITE
Springfield Armory NATIONAL HISTORIC SITE

By the Numbers

1978: Year the park was established

141: Acres in the park

1826: Year Lowell was incorporated

10,000: Number of looms in the mills in Lowell's heyday

$3.50: Top pay per week for a mill girl

4:30: Time in the morning factory bells woke up the workers

LOWELL
NATIONAL HISTORICAL PARK

PICTURED ROCKS
NATIONAL LAKESHORE

Lake Superior's Pictured Rocks was proclaimed the first national lakeshore in 1966. This is also the world's largest freshwater lake, and the coldest and deepest of the five Great Lakes. There are forty-two miles of shoreline here, and fifteen miles full of awesome rock formations on huge cliffs, some as high as two hundred feet.

And what mysterious-looking rocks they are! Made of sandstone, these rocks were carved by nature over the centuries into arches and caves. And many do look like pictures—a person's profile, say, or a castle: Half the fun is looking at the shapes and brilliant colors and making up your own stories about them. The colors come from different minerals inside the sandstone: Red and orange mean there's iron within; white signals limonite; black means manganese abounds; and green indicates copper.

Even larger than the rocks are the Grand Sable Dunes, formed over time by ice and wind—they're about three hundred feet high. This park is oddly shaped, following the contours of the shoreline, so the dunes and many other lakes, waterfalls, and beaches are accessible by car, and then a hike. The best way to see the rocks is from the water, since not all of the lakeshore is reachable by foot. There are boat cruises and sea kayaking, but be prepared: The water is extremely chilly.

There's plenty of wildlife here, but since visitors are so often out on the water, you have to keep a sharp eye out. If you do, you could be rewarded with sightings of moose, black bears, wolves, martens, skunks, red squirrels, and plenty more. So bring your camera!

AMAZING BUT TRUE!

A stone turret on the Miners Castle rock formation crumbled into the lake in 2006. This is the fifth large rockfall there in recent history. (There is still one turret left.)

RANGER FACT

Though the gray wolf is an endangered animal in the United States, you may occasionally see one loping along at Pictured Rocks.

The GREAT AMERICAN BIRDWATCH

SANDHILL CRANE

In the warmer months, you may see the male and female Sandhill Crane standing together, singing a love song. Large and gray, with as much as an eight-foot wingspan, the Sandhill Crane is often mistaken for a Blue Heron—but in flight, the crane's neck is extended, and the heron's is tucked into its chest. Fossils show the Sandhill Crane to be one of the oldest birds—about 2.5 million years old.

OTHER NATIONAL PARKS in MICHIGAN

Father Marquette
NATIONAL MEMORIAL
Isle Royale NATIONAL PARK
Keweenaw
NATIONAL HISTORICAL PARK
River Raisin
NATIONAL BATTLEFIELD PARK
Sleeping Bear Dunes
NATIONAL LAKESHORE

By the Numbers

1966: Year the park was established

73,236: Acres in the park

15: Miles of shoreline that feature Pictured Rocks

31,700: Area of Lake Superior in square miles (larger than New England if you left out Maine!)

55°F: Average August water temperature in Lake Superior

5: Park, in miles, at its widest point

By the Numbers

1975: Year the park was established

218,054: Acres in the park

344,000: Square miles of water in the park

175: Number of campsites in the park

9°F: Average temperature in International Falls in January

150: Black bears at the park, along with several packs of wolves

VOYAGEURS
NATIONAL PARK

You may have been to a water park before—but nothing like this!

Voyageurs National Park is named for the voyagers who worked as fur traders traveling in these waters in birch bark canoes way back in the seventeenth century. (*Voyageurs* is French for "voyagers" or "travelers.") Now these lakes are home to a national park that is almost completely made of water.

There are four major lakes here: Rainy Lake, Kabetogama Lake, Namakan Lake, and Sand Point Lake. Most visitors travel around and explore by canoe or kayak—you can even rent houseboats and stay aboard. If you want to camp here on the Kabetogama Peninsula, the only land portion in Voyageurs, you have to bring everything in your boat—better make sure you don't forget anything!

There is great fishing here, no matter what you are trying to catch. Depending on where you toss your line, you can hook smallmouth bass, largemouth bass, walleye, yellow perch, lake trout, lake whitefish, crappie, and much more. But northern Minnesota's summers are short. During the cold weather, you can cross-country ski, or snowmobile to where you want to go and enjoy the winter versions of the same fun, like ice fishing, snowshoe hiking, and winter camping!

RANGER FACT

The rock formations you see along the shores here are about as old as the earth's formation— 1 to 3 billion years old.

AMAZING BUT TRUE!

International Falls, the town that borders Canada and is Voyageurs' address, calls itself the "Icebox of the Nation." The record low temperature there is −55°F.

OTHER
NATIONAL PARKS
IN
MINNESOTA

Grand Portage
NATIONAL MONUMENT
Mississippi
NATIONAL RIVER
AND RECREATION AREA
Pipestone NATIONAL MONUMENT

The
GREAT AMERICAN
BIRDWATCH
LOON

The common Loon may look a lot like a duck to you, though its head is black and its beak much more pointed. But the Loon is a diver, and lots of fun to watch. It swims along and then suddenly it's plunged underwater in search of fish. And here's something unusual: Loon chicks ride on a parent's back!

By the Numbers

1899: Year the park was established

1,852.75: Acres in the park

1 million+: Visitors to the park annually

31: States that have built memorials in the park in their soldiers' memories

18,244: Soldiers buried in Vicksburg National Cemetery

12,954: Soldiers buried in Vickburg who remain unidentified

the GREAT AMERICAN BIRDWATCH

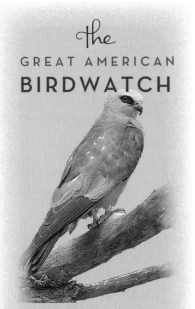

MISSISSIPPI KITE

The National Audubon Society has named the park and its environs an Important Bird Area, and one of the many specimens you'll see here is the Mississippi Kite, a smallish bird of prey. These birds eat mostly insects caught in flight, but will swoop in occasionally for a small rabbit or bird. At this point, kites are a protected species in this country: No touching or moving their nests or eggs is allowed.

VICKSBURG
NATIONAL MILITARY PARK

Vicksburg, Mississippi is the site of one of our Civil War's most important battles, a siege in 1863 that many historians say signaled the beginning of the end of the war. The Confederate Army's control of the city meant any traffic up the Mississippi River was impossible, as it served as a blockade for both travel and ammunition. It was imperative that the Union conquer Vicksburg. After forty-seven days and nearly twenty thousand dead, the Confederates surrendered.

This park is a memorial to all the men who fought in that war—North and South. A good place to start your visit is with the movie at the visitors' center. There is a sixteen-mile drive, which you can take by yourself or as part of a tour, with numerous stops that tell much about the strategy and battles that took place nearby before Vicksburg fell. There are well over a thousand memorials and remembrances here—many built by the states that lost soldiers. You'll also find cannons, trenches, and a cemetery. You can even see the USS *Cairo*, a gunboat sunk during the war that was dredged up in 1964 and is now on display.

And there's more than history to experience: While you're touring the park, you may run across all kinds of animals native to the American South, from alligators to armadillos, beavers to crayfish, plus snakes and bats galore.

RANGER FACT

At one point during the Civil War, General Ulysses S. Grant, who would later become president, tried to have his soldiers dig and widen the Mississippi to bypass Vicksburg, so the troops would have access to the river.

66 Vicksburg is the key. The war can never be brought to a close until that key is in our pocket. 99
—PRESIDENT ABRAHAM LINCOLN

OTHER
NATIONAL PARKS
In
MISSISSIPPI

Brices Cross Roads
NATIONAL BATTLEFIELD SITE
Natchez NATIONAL HISTORICAL PARK
Natchez Trace
NATIONAL SCENIC TRAIL
Natchez Trace PARKWAY
Tupelo NATIONAL BATTLEFIELD

OZARK
NATIONAL SCENIC RIVERWAYS

Get out your paddles, because the best thing in this park is all about floating through it. Ozark National Scenic Riverways is the first national park to protect a wild river system—those of the Current and Jacks Fork Rivers.

the
GREAT AMERICAN
BIRDWATCH

SWAINSON'S WARBLER

Swainson's Warbler is a tiny bird, only about five or six inches long, with an olive-brown back and a white chest. These warblers are endangered in this area, and since they nest in rivercane thickets, which look like bamboo, you may not even know they are here, but for their sharp, bright, six-note song. (Also, they fly south to Jamaica for the winter!)

AMAZING BUT TRUE!

Over 276 million gallons of water flow out of Big Spring, one of the country's largest, into the springs every day!

In fact, your entire visit here in the Riverways can happen on the water. There are more than 350 springs here—some of the largest in the world—and they make the rivers what they are: clear, beautiful, and clean. A spring is water that is forced up from underground, so they keep the river constantly moving. You can go out for an hour's drift, or stay on the rivers all day long.

There are more than three hundred caves here, too, but only one, Round Spring Cavern, offers a two-hour, ranger-led lantern tour. It's eerie and awesome and includes lots of hiking, so be prepared! There are also out-of-cave hikes, bluegrass concerts, and campfire activities, where you can learn about local history, wildlife, and maybe even some local ghosts.

Speaking of wildlife, there's plenty here to see. In the water you might spot beavers, muskrats, and minks, grotto salamanders in a cave, and venomous snakes, like the plentiful copperheads, pygmy rattlesnakes, and water moccasins. There are even tarantulas and scorpions around, so always keep your eyes open. If you're lucky, you may also see the Ozark hell-

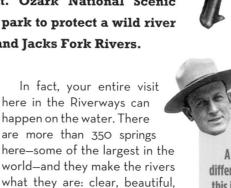

bender, a harmless salamander only found in the river's clear waters.

And if you ever have your fill of floating down the rivers, there's always horseback riding, fishing, camping, hunting, and more. Lots of folks say you can be in the park a whole week without ever going in the water!

OTHER
NATIONAL PARKS
IN
MISSOURI

George Washington Carver
NATIONAL MONUMENT
Harry S. Truman
NATIONAL HISTORIC SITE
Jefferson
NATIONAL EXPANSION MEMORIAL
Ulysses S. Grant
NATIONAL HISTORIC SITE
Wilson's Creek
NATIONAL BATTLEFIELD

By the Numbers

1964: Year the park was established

80,000: Acres in the park

1,300,000: Visitors to the park annually

300+: Caves in the park

350+: Springs is the park

58°F: Approximate average river temperature

70: tons of dissolved limestone in the water of Big Spring each day

FIELD TRIPS—CAMPFIRE PROGRAMS
NATURAL HISTORY TALKS & DISPLAYS
GENERAL INFORMATION

GLACIER
NATIONAL PARK
U.S. DEPARTMENT OF THE INTERIOR
NATIONAL PARK SERVICE

GLACIER
NATIONAL PARK

They call Montana "Big Sky" country, and if you look around, you can see why. Here in Glacier National Park, under the big sky, there were many glaciers—at least until about ten thousand years ago. When you look around, you can see the U-shaped valleys between mountain peaks that are the signature left by long-ago melted glaciers. There are still 25 active glaciers here today, but in 1850, there were 150—that's how fast our environment is changing!

GLACIER
NATIONAL PARK
1939

Hiking is the most popular activity in the park's million-plus acres. More than half the people who visit will explore one of the seven hundred miles of trails. There's some of the best fly-fishing in the country—though if you catch an endangered bull trout, you'll have to throw him back in! You can sightsee on the Red Jammers, awesome old buses that have been modernized to bring you around the park, including the famed Going-to-the-Sun Road, a spectacular fifty-mile feat of engineering that takes you across the entire park, and even over the Continental Divide. Be prepared, though: Sometimes parts of it are closed, even in the summer, because of the danger of avalanches.

While there are more than sixty species of animal in the park, there is only one mascot: the mountain goat! Though it *looks* more like a goat, it's a member of the cattle family, but with extra-large hooves so it can easily climb the steepest slopes of the Rocky Mountains. In the winter, mountain goats produce two layers of wool, and in the spring they rub themselves on nearby rocks to rid themselves of the extra warmth.

AMAZING BUT TRUE!

There are over 700 lakes in the park, but only 131 of them have been named!

By the Numbers

1910: Year the park was established

1,013,322: Acres in the park

2,000,000+: Visitors to the park annually

10,000: Years ago, when Native Americans first came to the Glacier area

10: Deaths by grizzly bear in the park since 1910

The GREAT AMERICAN BIRDWATCH

HARLEQUIN DUCK

Also called Clown Ducks, Painted Ducks, and Totem Ducks for the male's blue, brown, orange, and white markings, the Harlequin Duck is very common here in the park, though usually it's found mostly in streams and rocky ocean shorelines. Harlequin Ducks are great divers that walk along the bottom to feed on insects and mollusks, then pop back up like a cork to the surface.

DEPARTMENT OF THE INTERIOR, NATIONAL PARK SERVICE

THE NATIONAL PARKS
PRESERVE WILD LIFE

MADE BY WORKS PROGRESS ADMINISTRATION FEDERAL ART PROJECT NYC

By the Numbers

1966: Year the park was established

102,296: Acres in the park

200,000+: Visitors per year

71: Bighorn Lake's length, in miles

2,500: Depth, in feet, of Bighorn Canyon at Bull Elk Ridge

OTHER
NATIONAL PARKS
ıııııııııııı In ııııııııııııı
MONTANA

Big Hole NATIONAL BATTLEFIELD
Grant-Kohrs Ranch
NATIONAL HISTORIC SITE
Little Bighorn Battlefield
NATIONAL MONUMENT

RANGER FACT

Approximately 160 wild horses, as well as bighorn sheep, live in the 39,000-acre Pryor Mountain Wild Horse Range in Bighorn Canyon.

BIGHORN CANYON
NATIONAL RECREATION AREA

This is a story of how a plan to harness energy turned out to have a totally different use: fun!

In the 1960s, the government built Yellowtail Dam to harness energy from Bighorn River, and provide electricity and irrigate the surrounding region. Then, when the dam was built, the lake became a popular destination for boating and water sports. The only thing perhaps more popular is the trout fishing in the river below the dam! And there's also horseback riding (you might even spot wild horses galloping by), camping, hiking, and beautiful drives along the thousand-foot-drop canyon to enjoy.

AMAZING
BUT TRUE!
At a place called Sullivan's Knob here in the park, visitors can shout and hear themselves in a triple echo!

the
GREAT AMERICAN
BIRDWATCH
LAZULI BUNTING
The Lazuli Bunting is named for the bright blue gemstone, the lapis lazuli—the same color you'll find on this bird's head and back in the male of this species; the female is mostly brown and white.

AMAZING
BUT TRUE!

The law said
homesteaders were
required to put a
twelve-by-fourteen building
on their land. But, since it
didn't actually say twelve-
by-fourteen-*feet* anywhere
in the law, some put up
twelve-by-fourteen-*inch*
structures to meet
the rules!

HOMESTEAD NATIONAL MONUMENT OF AMERICA

Imagine if today someone said to your mom or dad, "Do you want 160 acres of free land?" Well, that's just what happened right here in Nebraska when the Homestead Act was passed in 1862. Thousands of people moved here, aiding the country's westward expansion to the Pacific Ocean. To earn the land, you had to build a cabin, farm the acres for five years, and pay an $18 filing fee. The act eventually transferred 270 million acres from the government to the people.

RANGER FACT

Some might say this site exists because of Daniel Freeman, a doctor and a Civil War veteran who was the very first person to file a claim under the Homestead Act on January 1, 1863. He eventually owned more than a thousand acres. He bragged about being the first homesteader so often that, upon his death in 1908, neighbors petitioned to erect a monument to him.

the GREAT AMERICAN BIRDWATCH

WESTERN MEADOWLARK

The Western Meadowlark is the state bird of Nebraska, and a familiar sight across the Plains states. Its long beak and the distinctive black V on its bright yellow chest make it easy to spot. Not surprisingly, the meadowlark eats seeds and grain, and makes its nest on the ground—sometimes complete with roof and tunnels!

This park is a celebration of the Homestead Act, and sits on some of the first land claimed back then by so-called homesteaders. There is a Heritage Homestead Center, with exhibits on agriculture, immigration, and more, and even an education center, where kids in classrooms from all over the country can go online and learn. You can also visit the Palmer-Epard cabin several miles away, and get an idea of how a whole family lived in a tiny fourteen-by-sixteen-foot home, far away from their old lives.

Before you leave, gaze out at the tallgrass prairie, and see the way the plains looked when the pioneers came out here to live. The National Park Service still mows, hays, and burns it regularly, just as the homesteaders would have done.

OTHER NATIONAL PARKS IN NEBRASKA

Agate Fossil Beds
NATIONAL MONUMENT

Chimney Rock
NATIONAL HISTORIC SITE
Lewis & Clark
NATIONAL HISTORIC TRAIL
National Underground Railroad:
Network to Freedom
Niobrara NATIONAL SCENIC RIVER
Scotts Bluff
NATIONAL MONUMENT

By the Numbers

1936: Year the park was established

195: Acres in the park

270,000,000: Acres of land given away under the Homestead Act

10: Percentage of the country that was given away to homesteaders

100: Acres of tallgrass on the site

In the Great Basin National Park, the elevations range from five thousand to thirteen thousand feet, allowing for a diversity of landforms, from hot deserts to damp caves to soaring mountains to a lone glacier. The highest high and the lowest low are the most interesting and fun places to visit. Take the scenic drive up thirteen thousand feet to the snow-capped Wheeler Peak. Some hike the last three thousand feet, a four-hour trip each way. And at the bottom of the basin, there are forty known caves. You can take a tour of Lehman's Caves and see stalactites, stalagmites, helictites, crazy limestone formations, and lots and lots of bats!

The unusual topography allows for eight hundred different plant species: Down near the visitors' center at Lehman's Caves, there are sagebrush, junipers, and saltbrush. Up at higher elevations are pine, aspen, fir, and spruce: A bristlecone pine that was nearly five thousand years old was cut down in 1964 for research purposes. And if you think that's old, there's the local Bonneville cutthroat trout, whose ancestors swam these waters sixteen thousand to eighteen thousand years ago.

By the Numbers

1986: Year the park was established

77,180: Acres in the park

13,063: Height, in feet, of Wheeler Peak

5,000,000: Years ago that Lehman Caves began to form

108°F: Highest recorded temperature in the park, in 1981

−26°F: Lowest recorded temperature in the park, in 1989

90: Length, in feet, of the Big Sagebrush's roots

60: Height, in feet, a mountain lion can drop and land running

9: Height, in feet, a kangaroo rat can jump when foraging for food

RANGER FACT

Because of the vastly different types of landscapes here, you'll see all kinds of animals, from jackrabbits, pygmy rabbits, and mountain cottontails down below to badgers, coyotes, and kit foxes in the higher elevations.

the GREAT AMERICAN BIRDWATCH

LONG-BILLED CURLEW

The Long-Billed Curlew has an extremely long beak, the better to forage for food—crabs, insects, whatever its bill can dig out. It's also called the "candlestick bird," and was once so common in the San Francisco area that the ballpark was named after the bird!

THE OTHER NATIONAL PARK In NEVADA

Lake Mead
NATIONAL RECREATION AREA

AMAZING
BUT TRUE!

Never heard of the state called Deseret? That's because it was never recognized by the U.S. government, even though the Mormons proposed it way back in 1849. It would have included most of Nevada and Utah, and encompassed Great Basin National Park.

GREAT
BASIN

WHITE
MOUNTAIN
NATIONAL FOREST

By the Numbers

1918: Year the forest was established

784,505: Acres in the forest

6,000,000+: Visitors per year

1,200: Miles of hiking trails

23: Campgrounds in the forest

60: Captive-bred Peregrine Falcons released from cliffs in the forest

6: Average number of fires a year

Have you ever been peak-bagging? It's an activity where hikers and mountaineers attempt to climb to the top of a certain collection of local mountains. Most of the one hundred highest ones in New Hampshire are here in the White Mountain National Forest.

If you like your sports a little less extreme, camping, fishing, and horseback riding are everywhere, of course—not to mention more than 100 miles of the Appalachian Trail, which spans nearly 2,200 miles from Georgia to Maine. The fishing is great here, and you'll see wild animals like black bear and moose: There's even a moose tour! However, the most famous sport in the White Mountains is skiing the fifty-five-foot-deep snow of Tuckerman Ravine.

The dangers of the mountain almost outshine its beauty. There is so much snow in the White Mountains—and it gets so cold—that people wait until late spring to ski Tuckerman. Skiers climb more than two miles up Mount Washington with all their gear to ski down this monster, which in places is as steep as fifty-five degrees! Each year, more than a thousand tons of ice form on the headwall of Tuckerman. In the spring it all comes down, often in pieces larger than cars. If that doesn't dissuade you, there are also avalanches. That said, it attracts some three thousands skiers a day between March and May.

RANGER FACT

Geocaching is very popular in the White Mountains. It is like a gigantic scavenger hunt using a GPS signal to find treasures. Instead of taking the find, you sign a logbook, like others before you, and go on to the next prize.

THE OTHER NATIONAL PARK In NEW HAMPSHIRE

Saint-Gaudens
NATIONAL HISTORIC SITE

the GREAT AMERICAN BIRDWATCH

BLACK-THROATED BLUE WARBLER

The Black-Throated Blue Warbler is a pretty little songbird, the male black-throated with a plump white belly and bright blue back. The female is olive-brown on top, with a light yellow belly. These birds love the cool forests in the summer for breeding, filled with insects to eat, then fly all the way to the Caribbean or Central America in the winter.

AMAZING BUT TRUE!

The meteorologists at the top of Mount Washington recorded winds of 231 mph in 1934. There is fog at the summit about 100 days of the year, hurricane-force winds more than 110 days of the year, and on January 22, 1985, the temperature was −55 degrees Fahrenheit! Some say it's the world's worst weather!

By the Numbers

1965: Year Ellis Island became part of the Statue of Liberty National Monument

5,000: Number of immigrants who came daily to Ellis Island at it busiest

12,000,000: Total number of immigrants who came to this country through Ellis Island

3,000,000: Visitors to Ellis Island a year now

40: Percentage of Americans who can trace an ancestor back to Ellis Island

2: Percentage of people who were sent back home from Ellis Island due to health and other problems

151: Height, in feet, of the Statue of Liberty from the top of the base to the top of the torch

3: Width, in feet, of the statue's mouth

ELLIS ISLAND
NATIONAL MONUMENT

Ellis Island is in New Jersey? Even though you take a ferry here from New York City, and it is in Upper New York Harbor, most of the island is considered part of New Jersey.

Long ago, Ellis Island was a tiny spot of just over three acres when the government decided to enlarge it to more than twenty-seven acres by adding landfill from the building of the New York City subway system. When the federal government took over immigration processing from the states, federal officials built a wooden building on Ellis Island, which opened in 1892. Annie Moore, a fifteen-year-old Irish girl, accompanied by her two brothers, were the very first immigrants to be processed at Ellis Island.

Five years later the building burned down. That is when the fireproof building that is now the Immigration Museum was constructed. There are still more than thirty other buildings on the island—most of them in shambles—such as hospitals, quarantine quarters, and a ferry terminal.

A visitor today can listen to stories on headphones from real immigrants about their own experiences, see photographs, read news clippings, and view possessions left behind. You can even research your own ancestors and see if they first set foot on American soil on Ellis Island.

The ferry also stops at Liberty Island, where you can see the Statue of Liberty, a gift from France that is a beacon of hope for people coming to America since 1886. The statue has a steel frame and a copper skin, a metal which turns green over time. It was built to be able to sway in the harbor's winds. The torch can move up to six inches in fifty mile-per-hour winds.

AMAZING BUT TRUE!

On April 17, 1907, 11,741 immigrants were processed at Ellis Island—the most ever in a single day.

RANGER FACT

Right here on the island is an ever-growing Wall of Honor, where people can have their ancestors' names inscribed, so they and *their* descendants can remember them forever.

the GREAT AMERICAN BIRDWATCH

GULL

Before you even get to Ellis Island, you may see gulls following behind the ferry, catching its draft and sniffing for food! They are related to the tern, and, as almost any beachgoer knows, they're scavengers that will steal food at a moment's notice. Usually white and gray, a gull can be from about a foot long to around thirty inches. They are very sociable, at ease both with other gulls and around humans—and human food!

OTHER NATIONAL PARKS In NEW JERSEY

Great Egg Harbor
SCENIC AND RECREATIONAL RIVER
Morristown
NATIONAL HISTORICAL PARK
New Jersey
COASTAL HERITAGE TRAIL ROUTE
Pinelands NATIONAL RESERVE
Thomas Edison
NATIONAL HISTORICAL PARK

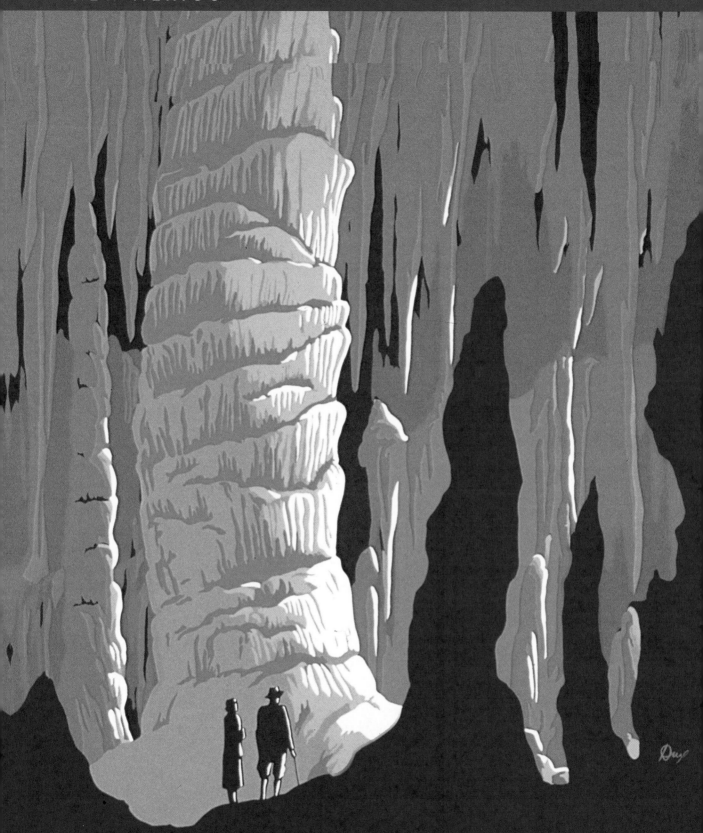

SEE AMERICA
UNITED STATES TRAVEL BUREAU

MADE BY WORKS PROGRESS ADMINISTRATION   FEDERAL ART PROJECT NYC

CARLSBAD CAVERNS
NATIONAL PARK

By the Numbers

1930: Year the park was established

46,766.45: Acres in the park

300,000+: Visitors per year

357,469: Caves in the park

17: Species of bats in the park

600: Mosquitoes a bat can eat in one hour

1: Days the park is closed each year (Christmas)

RANGER FACT

Make sure you see the Bat Flight, when 400,000 Brazilian free-tail bats fly out of the caves at sundown, in search of tons and tons of insects for dinner.

As a young boy, Jim White (1882–1946) found the most incredible caverns near Carlsbad, New Mexico. He went there all the time, bringing along his homemade ladder: Most folks he told didn't even believe there *were* any caverns. And when he grew up, Jim White became . . . a park ranger!

You can walk into a huge, yawning hole in the caverns, or take an elevator down to the bottom. (As you do, think of sixteen-year-old Jim White, discovering all this, bit by bit!) These are limestone caves, left from an inland sea hundreds of millions of years ago. They have lots of crazy names, like Bat Cave, Chocolate High, Lake of the Clouds, Mystery Room, Papoose Room, and Spider Cave. There's even one named Balloon Ballroom, because it was so high scientists reached the top by floating balloons up inside it!

the GREAT AMERICAN BIRDWATCH

CAVE SWALLOW

What else would you expect to find here but the Cave Swallow? Short-beaked and quite dull in color, except for some orange on the throat, Cave Swallows alternate their flying with several quick wingbeats, followed by a graceful glide. Carlsbad Caverns is one of their favorite American homes.

AMAZING BUT TRUE!

There used to be many more bats in the caverns than there are today—so many that there were companies that collected guano (that's a scientific term for bat poop!) to sell as fertilizer.

CHACO
CULTURE
NATIONAL HISTORICAL PARK

From AD 850 until 1250, Chaco was the bustling center of Pueobloan culture. The Chacoans carefully laid out the area for meeting and trading their wares, which included baskets, turquoise, and beads.

Their massive great houses were architectural marvels. Built from sandstone blocks from mountains as far as 50 miles away, they had anywhere from two hundred to seven hundred rooms. People from all over gathered here to share ceremonies, traditions, and knowledge. Gradually, Chaco became less important to the culture and was abandoned. You can take a tour or even ride a bike on a nine-mile loop and see these fascinating ruins. Don't worry too much about the native animals: Though there are coyotes and pronghorn and elk, visitors rarely see them.

By the Numbers

1966: Year designated as a national park

33,977.8: Acres in the park

15: Number of major complexes that were built here

50: Years of drought that are thought to have driven out the Chacoans

RANGER FACT

In ancient times, the Chaco Canyon was at the end of a large inland sea. Today, visitors have found fossil clam shells, shark teeth, and other animals in the canyon rocks.

the GREAT AMERICAN BIRDWATCH

CANYON TOWHEE

The Canyon Towhee can be seen in the brush; it is brown, plump, and long-tailed, and blends into its background so well that you may hardly notice one. They can be lazy, too: Look for them pecking insects from your car grille, and then scurrying under the car when you approach!

AMAZING BUT TRUE!
These Chacoan pueblos remained the largest buildings in North America until the 1800s.

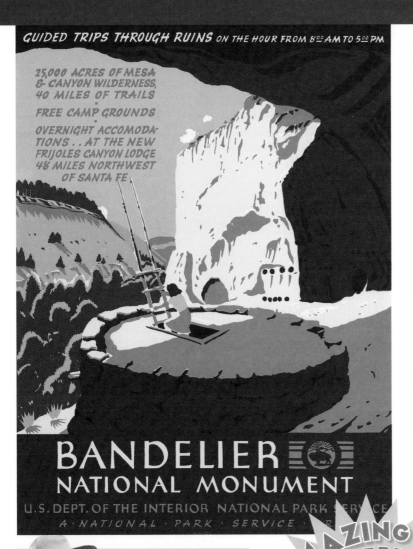

GUIDED TRIPS THROUGH RUINS ON THE HOUR FROM 8:00 AM TO 5:00 PM

25,000 ACRES OF MESA & CANYON WILDERNESS, 40 MILES OF TRAILS

· FREE CAMP GROUNDS

· OVERNIGHT ACCOMODATIONS .. AT THE NEW FRIJOLES CANYON LODGE 48 MILES NORTHWEST OF SANTA FE

BANDELIER
NATIONAL MONUMENT
U.S. DEPT. OF THE INTERIOR NATIONAL PARK SERVICE
A · NATIONAL · PARK · SERVICE · P

RANGER FACT

This park is named after Alfred Bandelier, a Swiss anthropologist who studied this area of New Mexico and its cultures.

OTHER
NATIONAL PARKS
In
NEW MEXICO

Aztec Ruins NATIONAL MONUMENT
Capulin Volcano NATIONAL MONUMENT
El Malpais NATIONAL MONUMENT
El Morro NATIONAL MONUMENT
Fort Union NATIONAL MONUMENT
Gila Cliff Dwelling NATIONAL MONUMENT
Old Spanish NATIONAL HISTORIC TRAIL
Pecos NATIONAL HISTORIC PARK
Petroglyph NATIONAL MONUMENT
Salinas Pueblo Missions NATIONAL MONUMENT
White Sands NATIONAL MONUMENT

AMAZING

BUT TRUE!

On some of the walls here, you will see petroglyphs, which are pictures ancient inhabitants carved out of the rocks.

the
GREAT AMERICAN
BIRDWATCH
WESTERN TANAGER

Some are now saying the Western Tanager is actually part of the cardinal family, and with its bright coloring, that would be no surprise. Females have a yellow head; males a red head and yellow-and-black back. They will stay in Bandelier only for the warm summer months.

By the Numbers

1916: Year Bandelier was designated a national monument

33,677: Acres in the park

23,367: Acres designated as a wilderness area

300,000: Visitors annually

70+: Miles of trails in the park

BANDELIER
NATIONAL MONUMENT

People roamed this part of what is now New Mexico as far back as ten thousand years ago. In order to survive, they would follow the wildlife that they could hunt and eat, and that was plentiful here.

Even now you can see elk, mountain lions, and mule deer. Around AD 1150, when the Chacoans left their pueblos, Pueblo people began to build homes here. They lived in this area about four hundred years before moving closer to the Rio Grande. But they left thousands of pueblos behind here amid the canyons and mesas. Walk the Main Loop Trail, just over a mile at the bottom of Frijoles Canyon, and see cliff dwellings, small ladders left behind and ancient pueblos.

By the Numbers

3,392: Acres in the park

1938: Year the park was established

2: Number of days the battles lasted—but almost **3** weeks apart

1,500: Number of men the British lost

800: Number of men the Americans lost

SARATOGA
NATIONAL HISTORICAL PARK

You might expect that the first big victory of the American Revolutionary War took place in somewhere like Boston, but it was right here, at the Battle of Saratoga. The colonies declared themselves independent in 1776, but the British were not willing to let go so easily—and it looked like the king's men might be winning, until the battles that took place near Saratoga. Not only did they give our soldiers some much-needed confidence, but it convinced other countries to support us and join our fight, most importantly France.

RANGER FACT

There is a monument to the traitor Benedict Arnold, who helped General Gates fight here—though it doesn't even have his name inscribed on it!

Much of the combat that took place here between British General John Burgoyne's men and our own General Horatio Gates's troops involved men shooting at each other from very short distances, on a piece of land only four square miles. You can tour; walk or ride bikes around the battlefield; see the Schuyler House, the country home of General Philip Schuyler, who also helped win these battles; and check out the Saratoga Monument. The newest part of the park is called Victory Woods, where the British encamped before the battle.

Throughout the year, there are lots of special events: reenactments of the battles, a day at the Schuyler House where you can see how people lived in the eighteenth century, programs especially for kids to learn about what it was like to be young in colonial times, and much more. But some things never change: As always, from Revolutionary War days until today, you will see deer everywhere, sprinting around the park.

AMAZING BUT TRUE!

Young boys—sometimes as young as twelve—fought as soldiers in the Revolutionary War.

the GREAT AMERICAN BIRDWATCH
SHARP-SHINNED HAWKS

Sharp-Shinned Hawks—or "sharpies" as they are called—are the smallest hawks in North America, about a foot long at their largest, with a wingspan of only two feet. This doesn't stop them from catching even tinier birds as food, often swooping down on them in flight. Reptiles, insects, mice, and frogs are also on the menu!

OTHER NATIONAL PARKS In NEW YORK

African Burial Ground NATIONAL MONUMENT
Castle Clinton NATIONAL MONUMENT
Eleanor Roosevelt NATIONAL HISTORIC SITE
Ellis Island NATIONAL MONUMENT
Erie Canalway NATIONAL HERITAGE CORRIDOR
Federal Hall NATIONAL MEMORIAL
Fire Island NATIONAL SEASHORE
Fort Stanwix NATIONAL MONUMENT
Gateway NATIONAL RECREATION AREA
General Grant NATIONAL MONUMENT
Governors Island NATIONAL MONUMENT
Hamilton Grange NATIONAL MONUMENT
Home of Franklin D. Roosevelt NATIONAL HISTORIC SITE
Martin Van Buren NATIONAL HISTORIC SITE
National Parks of New York Harbor
Sagamore Hill NATIONAL HISTORIC SITE
Saint Paul's Church NATIONAL HISTORIC
Statue of Liberty NATIONAL MONUMENT
Theodore Roosevelt Birthplace NATIONAL HISTORIC SITE
Theodore Roosevelt Inaugural NATIONAL HISTORIC SITE
Vanderbilt Mansion NATIONAL HISTORIC SITE
Women's Rights NATIONAL HISTORICAL PARK

When is a park not a park? When it's a road trip!

The Blue Ridge Parkway is a national parkway and all-American road. It runs south to north, all the way from the Great Smoky Mountains National Park in North Carolina to Waynesboro, Virginia—nearly five hundred miles. And this is no raceway: The speed limit is never more than forty-five miles per hour, so you won't miss a bit of the beautiful countryside.

More than a half century in the making, this highway mostly winds through the Blue Ridge Mountains, which are part of the Appalachians. And they really do look blue! Scientists say hydrocarbons released into the atmosphere from the forest give the air a bluish haze from afar. Called "America's favorite drive," the parkway allows you to stop and experience history along the way. Native Americans were longtime inhabitants of these parts, as were early European settlers. There are farm buildings you can visit, and museums where you can learn about Native American culture—in fact, part of the parkway passes right through the Cherokee Indian Reservation.

But maybe the most fun is to take time to see and find things just off the road: fishing, picnicking, tubing, and white-water rafting, foliage in the fall, and lots more. Because sometimes it's great to slow down and enjoy the ride!

RANGER FACT

People come from all over to see the wildflowers in the fields off the road. In spring and summer, the blooms change almost daily, with daisies, coreopsis, yellow yarrow, milkweed, rhododendron azalea, and plenty more.

AMAZING BUT TRUE!

Known as the "Crown of the Blue Ridge," Blowing Rock offers breathtaking views 4,090 feet above John's River Gorge. Strong winds return light objects thrown into the gorge.

By the Numbers

1936: Year the park was established

469.1: Length, in miles, of highway

19,000,000: Approximate number of visitors annually

6,684: Height, in feet, of Mount Mitchell

100: Miles the Appalachian Trail parallels the parkway

100: Species of trees along the parkway, as many as are found in all of Europe

2: Types of poisonous snakes in the park—the copperhead and timber rattler

The GREAT AMERICAN BIRDWATCH

BOBOLINK

The Bobolink can be seen up and down the parkway; look for a blackbird who seems like it's been in a snowstorm, what with a white cap, and some white on its back. Bobolinks love to live in an open field, finding insects and seeds on the ground. They have a chirpy call, which many think actually sounds like "bob-oh-LINK."

OTHER NATIONAL PARKS In NORTH CAROLINA

Cape Hatteras
NATIONAL SEASHORE
Cape Lookout
NATIONAL SEASHORE
Carl Sandburg Home
NATIONAL HISTORIC SITE
Fort Raleigh
NATIONAL HISTORIC SITE
Guilford Courthouse
NATIONAL MILITARY PARK
Moores Creek
NATIONAL BATTLEFIELD
Wright Brothers
NATIONAL MEMORIAL

BLUE RIDGE
PARKWAY

THEODORE ROOSEVELT
NATIONAL PARK

A place called the "Badlands" doesn't sound like much fun to visit, but it is! Still, you might wonder how it got its name. This land isn't easy to travel: The Lakota Indians called these areas *mako sica* and, later, French fur trappers named them *les mauvaises terres*. Both terms mean "bad lands." In many places, when you gaze around, it looks like what you might imagine a moonscape would look like: rocky, bare, and barren.

But Theodore Roosevelt made this area famous, when he came here in 1883 to hunt buffalo. He fell in love with the landscape, which also has grassy plains, mountains, and lots of wildlife, and returned here many times, even investing in the Maltese Cross Ranch on his very first trip. Roosevelt's visits were long ago, but there is still plenty of animal life here to astound you: bison, rattlesnakes, prairie dogs, elk, wild horses, mule deer, bighorn sheep, and more.

The park is actually split into three totally different sections—the North Unit, near Watford City; the South Unit, near Medora; and Roosevelt's Elkhorn Ranch in the middle. They are connected by the Maah Daah Hey Trail, Mandan Indian for "an area that will be around for a long time." It's a famous and incredible biking trail, but if you'd rather, there's kayaking, horseback riding, and backcountry hiking and camping, too. The sky is so dark at night, and it's so far north, that occasionally you can see even the northern lights.

> 66 I grow very fond of this place, and it certainly has a desolate, grim beauty of its own, that has a curious fascination for me. 99
> —THEODORE ROOSEVELT

OTHER
NATIONAL PARKS
In
NORTH DAKOTA

Fort Union Trading Post
NATIONAL HISTORIC SITE
Knife River Indian Villages
NATIONAL HISTORIC SITE

AMAZING
BUT TRUE!

The whole park has a wire fence to protect the wildlife—it keeps wild horses, cattle, and bison in the park, where they belong; but there are specially constructed points in the fence to let other animals come and go as they please!

By the Numbers

70,466.89: Acres, in three separate units, in the park

1947: Year the park was established as the first and only memorial park

1978: Year the park was renamed a national park

96: Length, in miles, of the Maah Daah Hey Trail

10: Diameter, in feet, of the red, round rocks known as concretions

60,000,000: Number of years ago the trees of the petrified forest lived

70–110: Wild horses in the park

By the Numbers

1978: Year the park was established; also the year the Northern Mariana Islands became a commonwealth in political union with the United States

133: Acres in the park

15: Number of islands comprising the Northern Mariana Islands

179.01: Square mileage of all Northern Mariana Islands

1,000: Troops out the **30,000** Japanese soldiers still alive at the end of the battle of Saipan

In the middle of the Pacific Ocean, much farther west even than Hawaii, are the Northern Mariana Islands. On an island named Saipan, one of the most decisive battles of World War II was fought. Many historians will tell you it was the most important battle fought in the Pacific, and that it turned the corner for the United States in its drive to defeat Japan.

NORTHERN MARIANA ISLANDS
AMERICAN MEMORIAL PARK

RANGER FACT

The battle was over when a Japanese commander committed ritual suicide, called *seppuku*.

This park is dedicated to the more than five thousand people who were killed here—soldiers, marines, pilots, military personnel, and island civilians. At the Court of Honor and Flag Circle, those names are inscribed for us to remember their sacrifice. But the park is also a living memorial, where visitors and the local community can visit the wetlands and mangrove forest, bike, swim, picnic, run, and generally enjoy this tropical paradise.

The GREAT AMERICAN BIRDWATCH

NIGHTINGALE REED-WARBLER

Found only here in the islands, this bird is critically endangered; only about two thousand remain, the rest have been destroyed by the brown tree snake. Known on the island as the Ga'Ga' Karisu, they love the wetlands and feed on snails, lizards, and insects. And since they're nightingales, of course, they often sing at night.

AMAZING BUT TRUE! The coconut crab found here is often as large as twelve inches across with a three-foot leg span!

By the Numbers

25.38: Acres in the park

1936: Year the park was established

200,000: Visitors annually

352: Height, in feet, of the memorial column

5: Miles the monument is from the Canadian border

RANGER FACT

As a reminder that people from both sides of the conflict die in war, the bodies of three American and three British officers lie beneath this monument.

PERRY'S VICTORY

AND INTERNATIONAL PEACE MEMORIAL

This park is in the odd-sounding town of Put-in-Bay, Ohio, and is not so easy to get to: Only a plane, boat, or ferry will get you there. And coming in by boat, perhaps you can almost picture Commodore Oliver Hazard Perry at the Battle of Lake Erie— because this is where he won the most important naval battle of the War of 1812. And that's why this gigantic column, the International Peace Memorial, is here: It commemorates the peace that has thrived ever since that war among the United States, Great Britain, and Canada.

AMAZING BUT TRUE!

The border between the United States and Canada is the longest undefended border in the world.

By the Numbers

32,947.07: Acres in the park

2000: Year the park was established

2,500,000: Approximate number of visitors annually

22: Miles of the Cuyahoga River that flow through the park

70: Waterfalls in the park

AMAZING BUT TRUE!

Mules used to walk the Towpath Trail to pull the boats down the canal. President James Garfield was a former "mule boy" himself, leading the mules along!

the GREAT AMERICAN BIRDWATCH

YELLOW WARBLER

The Yellow Warbler's song is as sunny as the male's plumage. Its bright yellow feathers may also be why they are so easy to spot by unfriendly neighbors like rats, reptiles, even foxes. In certain parts of the world, this species, which feeds mostly on insects, is given about a 50/50 chance of not being devoured themselves.

CUYAHOGA VALLEY NATIONAL PARK

This is one of the most visited parks in the country, and that may be because of something you haven't considered: Two huge cities—Cleveland and Akron, Ohio—are both nearby. The four million people who live within a half-hour's drive of the park can enjoy the Cuyahoga, a U-shaped river that flows both north and south for twenty-two miles in the valley.

The Ohio & Erie Canal runs through the park: It was built *by hand* in the early 1800s to connect the more than three hundred miles between the Ohio River and Lake Erie. Soon enough, the railroad arrived and the canal was no longer used for commerce, but as a water source for local communities. Nowadays, you can take incredible boat rides down parts of the canal, see rushing waterfalls, and bike or hike along the Towpath Trail, which runs more than eighty miles along the canal, twenty within the park.

There's the famous Blossom Music Center, Boy and Girl Scout camps, skiing, and lots more here. You'll find plenty of wildlife here, too; beavers, muskrats, minks, bald eagles, and raccoons are just a few critters you'll see scurrying around!

RANGER FACT

Cuyahoga means "crooked river" in Mohawk.

OTHER NATIONAL PARKS In OHIO

David Berger NATIONAL MEMORIAL
Dayton Aviation Heritage NATIONAL HISTORICAL PARK
First Ladies NATIONAL HISTORIC SITE
Hopewell Culture NATIONAL HISTORICAL PARK
James A. Garfield NATIONAL HISTORIC SITE
William Howard Taft NATIONAL HISTORIC SITE

AMAZING
BUT TRUE!

More than 2,400 acres in this park are underwater!

CHICKASAW
NATIONAL RECREATION AREA

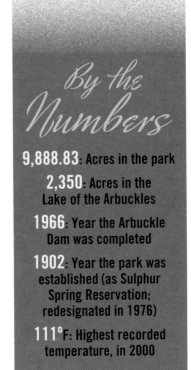

PLATT NATIONAL PARK 1939

Water has always been the attraction here, though it wasn't always called Chickasaw National Recreation Area. Early in the twentieth century, the government bought some land from the Chicasaw Indians to protect the mineral and freshwater springs. With the addition of more acreage, it became Platt National Park. In 1966, a huge human-made lake was built as a result of constructing the Arbuckle Dam and the Lake of the Arbuckles became one of the best fishing spots in the state, especially famous for bass. A decade later, the Platt and the Lake of the Arbuckles combined and took on its present name, in honor of the Chickasaw nation, who cherished and lived on this land for so many centuries.

RANGER FACT
When the Chickasaw first sold the land to the government, a special agreement was made that the park must not charge admission. That still holds true today.

the GREAT AMERICAN BIRDWATCH

RED-HEADED WOODPECKER
If the Red-Headed Woodpecker looks familiar, it's because he resembles Woody Woodpecker from the cartoons—without the laugh! These birds are easy to spot with their bright head and white belly, and though they will catch insects to eat in the air or on the ground, it's their rat-a-tat-tat pecking on a tree trunk for food that we so often hear and recognize. This bird is so famous he's even been pictured on a two-cent postage stamp!

You can explore this park in two ways: indoors or out! If you stop at the Travertine Nature Center, you can learn from the rangers about the park's history and view reptiles, birds, amphibians, and other animals on display. Or you can follow a trail to the Little Niagara waterfall, formed by one of a series of dams constructed along Travertine Creek. The creek tumbles over seventy-five natural rockfalls and down six human-made dams as it winds along its 2½-mile course to Pavilion Springs. You can visit the scenic Lincoln Bridge, dedicated in 1909 on the centennial of Abraham Lincoln's birth. It's the best of both worlds!

OTHER NATIONAL PARKS In OKLAHOMA
Oklahoma City NATIONAL MEMORIAL
Washita Battlefield NATIONAL HISTORIC SITE

By the Numbers
9,888.83: Acres in the park
2,350: Acres in the Lake of the Arbuckles
1966: Year the Arbuckle Dam was completed
1902: Year the park was established (as Sulphur Spring Reservation; redesignated in 1976)
111°F: Highest recorded temperature, in 2000

AMAZING BUT TRUE!

Mount Hood is what's known as a "sleeping volcano," and although there have been several minor eruptions, some scientists believe we may see a major event in this century.

MOUNT HOOD

NATIONAL FOREST

This is the go-to spot for mountain climbers: Mount Hood is the third most-climbed mountain in the world (Mount Fuji in Japan and Mount Monadnock in New Hampshire vie for first and second place)! There is fun to be had all year round at Mount Hood: great skiing and snowboarding at both the Mount Hood Meadows Ski Resort and the Timberline Lodge (the only year-round ski area in North America), and rafting, boating, fishing, hunting, and horseback riding in the warmer months. There are over twelve hundred miles of hiking trails. Animal life gets scarcer the higher you climb, but you may spot red foxes, wolves, chipmunks, or even a bear.

The Barlow Road, located here as well, is an important part of American history. Pioneers coming from the East could travel all the way from Missouri on what came to be known as the Oregon Trail, but until Sam Barlow built the last part of the trail in 1846, covered wagons could not get over the Cascades. Barlow built this road around the southern slopes of Mount Hood, and you can still hike, drive, and camp here today.

the GREAT AMERICAN BIRDWATCH

STELLER'S JAY

Steller's Jay is a much-sighted bird out West, similar to the common Blue Jay but with a black head. You'll often see Stellar's Jays in flocks of ten or more, and they are what's called omnivores: They will eat seeds, small animals, plants—just about anything!

CRATER LAKE
NATIONAL PARK

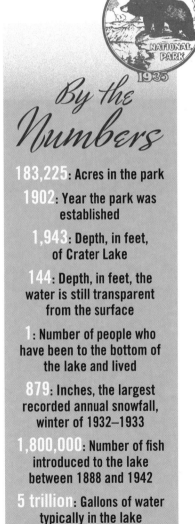

Picture the deepest lake in the entire United States, surrounded by two-thousand-foot-high cliffs, and you can begin to imagine the majesty of Crater Lake. This is not your usual kind of lake, however: It was formed by a violent volcanic eruption more than 7,500 years ago, which left a *caldera*, which is the hole made when Mount Mazama collapsed after an eruption. This clean blue lake is filled with nothing but rainwater and snowfall, so it is one of the clearest in the world.

The park is so diverse that you can take a snowshoe hike in some places—there's often snow still on the ground in the summertime—while hiking, fishing, swimming, and exploring the many types of wildflowers elsewhere! And don't miss Rim Drive—just as it sounds, you can follow this road completely around the caldera rim.

By the Numbers

183,225: Acres in the park

1902: Year the park was established

1,943: Depth, in feet, of Crater Lake

144: Depth, in feet, the water is still transparent from the surface

1: Number of people who have been to the bottom of the lake and lived

879: Inches, the largest recorded annual snowfall, winter of 1932–1933

1,800,000: Number of fish introduced to the lake between 1888 and 1942

5 trillion: Gallons of water typically in the lake

OTHER NATIONAL PARKS In OREGON

John Day Fossil Beds NATIONAL MONUMENT
Lewis and Clark NATIONAL HISTORICAL PARK
Oregon Caves NATIONAL MONUMENT

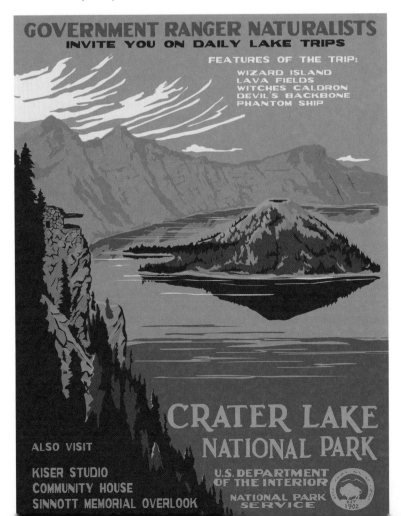

GOVERNMENT RANGER NATURALISTS
INVITE YOU ON DAILY LAKE TRIPS

FEATURES OF THE TRIP:
WIZARD ISLAND
LAVA FIELDS
WITCHES CALDRON
DEVIL'S BACKBONE
PHANTOM SHIP

CRATER LAKE NATIONAL PARK

ALSO VISIT
KISER STUDIO
COMMUNITY HOUSE
SINNOTT MEMORIAL OVERLOOK

U.S. DEPARTMENT OF THE INTERIOR
NATIONAL PARK SERVICE

By the
Numbers

5,990.39: Acres in the park

1895: Year established
as a park

75,000: Number of
Confederate troops involved
at Gettysburg

95,000: Number of Union
troops involved at Gettysburg

51,000: Approximate
number of casualties suffered
in the Battle of Gettysburg

1,400+: Number of
memorials and markers
in the park

GETTYSBURG NATIONAL MILITARY PARK

The blood of more than 51,000 soldiers soaked the ground of Gettysburg, the site of what was perhaps America's most famous battle. For three days, July 1–3, 1863, at the height of the Civil War, the fighting continued until General Robert E. Lee turned back to the south with his troops. It was the bloodiest battle of the war, where churches, private homes, town halls, and nearly every building available was turned into a makeshift hospital and every farm field or garden was a graveyard.

AMAZING BUT TRUE!

The first visitors to the Gettysburg battlefield arrived just days after the battle; they were the relatives of the slain, searching for their loved ones.

Start your visit at the Museum and Visitors' Center, where you can see interactive exhibits and war relics. One of the highlights here is the Gettysburg Cyclorama, which is a 360-degree painting that details Pickett's Charge, the assault that likely lost the war for the Confederacy.

Then you can explore the battlefield on your own by car, or go with a guide. There are evening campfires, living history groups and concerts, and battle reenactments. The rangers even have a program where kids can "enlist" in the army, and learn a little about what being a soldier was like at Gettysburg.

OTHER NATIONAL PARKS In PENNSYLVANIA

Allegheny Portage Railroad
NATIONAL HISTORIC SITE
Delaware & Lehigh
NATIONAL HERITAGE CORRIDOR
Delaware
NATIONAL SCENIC RIVER
Delaware Water Gap
NATIONAL RECREATION AREA
Edgar Allan Poe
NATIONAL HISTORIC SITE
Eisenhower
NATIONAL HISTORIC SITE
Flight 93
NATIONAL MEMORIAL
Fort Necessity
NATIONAL BATTLEFIELD
Friendship Hill
NATIONAL HISTORIC SITE
Gloria Dei Church
NATIONAL HISTORIC SITE
Hopewell Furnace
NATIONAL HISTORIC SITE
Independence
NATIONAL HISTORICAL PARK
Johnstown Flood
NATIONAL MEMORIAL
Steamtown
NATIONAL HISTORIC SITE
Thaddeus Kosciuszko
NATIONAL MEMORIAL
Upper Delaware
SCENIC AND RECREATIONAL RIVER
Valley Forge
NATIONAL HISTORICAL PARK

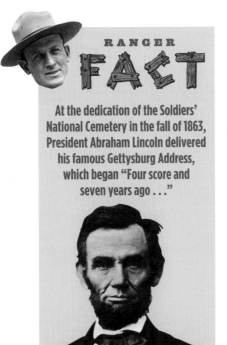

RANGER FACT

At the dedication of the Soldiers' National Cemetery in the fall of 1863, President Abraham Lincoln delivered his famous Gettysburg Address, which began "Four score and seven years ago . . ."

the GREAT AMERICAN BIRDWATCH

AMERICAN ROBIN

It seems natural to find a bird as simple as the American Robin here in a place so important to our country's history. This orange-breasted bird is one of the first you'll hear singing in the morning, and is common in farmland like this, and even in cities, hunting caterpillars, fruits, and berries.

EL YUNQUE
NATIONAL FOREST

By the Numbers

28,002: Acres in the park

1903: Year the park was established

1,250,000: Visitors annually

1,065: Height, in feet, of El Toro, park's (and Puerto Rico's) tallest mountain

200+: Inches of rainfall here annually—that's **100** billion gallons of water!

12,000: Eggs laid at one time by the park's Fathead Minnow—females may spawn 12 times a season!

70–95: Percentage of all the park's seeds dispersed by the Antillean ghost-faced bat

30: Height, in feet, of the tree fern

THE OTHER
NATIONAL PARK
In
PUERTO RICO

San Juan NATIONAL HISTORIC SITE

Lots of visitors come to Puerto Rico for the beautiful beaches and a fun Caribbean vacation, but hidden here in the mountains is the only tropical rain forest in the United States. Located on the mountain slopes, it's filled with waterfalls, rivers, lush vegetation (you'll see ferns way taller than you are!), and unusual wildlife, like large tree snails and the famous coqui frog: It's as tiny as a quarter and sings all night long.

RANGER FACT

A person born in Puerto Rico is called a *Borinqueño*.

the
GREAT AMERICAN
BIRDWATCH
PUERTO RICAN PARROT

The Puerto Rican Parrot is an endangered species of Amazon Parrot found only here on the island. There are fewer than two hundred in captivity, and if you catch sight of one in El Yunque, you will have seen one of about only forty remaining in the wild. Mostly bright green, with some red above the beak, this parrot is an herbivore, which means he's a vegetarian!

Drive up the mountains and stop first at El Portal Visitors' Center to learn about rain forests and conservation before you start your own exploration. A walkway set sixty feet above ground allows you to see the tops of the trees. Perhaps you'll glimpse flocks of Orange-Fronted Parakeets. Then go on to enjoy hiking, picnicking, camping—even swim under a waterfall.

BLOCK ISLAND
NATIONAL WILDLIFE REFUGE

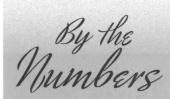

This craggy little island—it's smaller than ten square miles—off the coast of Rhode Island's mainland is a summer paradise for tourists and vacationers. But in the cold winter months, only about a thousand people live here! For humans, it's a great place to swim, fish, and enjoy the summertime. And if you're a bird-watcher, you can hardly find a better place.

RANGER FACT

This may come as no surprise, but Block Island is home to the largest gull colony in the state.

This is a paradise for birds, too, well past the summer months. When birds migrate south for the winter, they mostly travel along what's called a "flyway," which often follows the eastern shoreline in this part of the country. But sometimes the first-timers lose sight of the mainland and stop over here on Block Island and its National Wildlife Refuge to rest and eat. They are often dehydrated, and the lakes, ponds, and ripe berries here may just save many of their lives. It's one of the most famous bird habitats in the United States, and it's great fun to see and hear these aviary visitors, because many of them are songbirds—more than seventy different species.

OTHER NATIONAL PARKS In RHODE ISLAND

Blackstone River Valley
NATIONAL HERITAGE CORRIDOR
Roger Williams NATIONAL MEMORIAL
Touro Synagogue
NATIONAL HISTORIC SITE

By the Numbers

127: Acres in the refuge

1973: Year Block Island was established as a wildlife refuge

12: Distance, in miles, Block Island is from the mainland

15: Number of rare or endangered species that live on the island

1: Town on all of Block Island, called New Shoreham

FORT SUMTER
NATIONAL MONUMENT

AMAZING *BUT* **TRUE!**
Although no one was killed at the Battle of Fort Sumter, one Union soldier died when he was injured by a cannonball explosion.

American military history made its mark here; perhaps the most famous moments were when the Confederacy fired on Union soldiers on April 12, 1861 at Fort Sumter. These were the opening shots of the American Civil War.

But Fort Sumter was not the first site built to protect Charleston. In 1776, Fort Moultrie (also on the site of Fort Sumter National Monument) was in the process of being built to protect this valuable harbor when the British attacked from the sea. What the British didn't count on was that their cannonballs would bounce right off the soft, spongy palmetto logs the fort was made of! They retreated several hours later.

After touring Fort Moultrie, stop at the Visitors' Education Center and learn more about what led the North and the South into this terrible war, and see the tattered flag that flew over Fort Sumter on both April 12, 1861 and April 14, 1865, when the Union Army regained control of the fort. Then take a ferry over to Fort Sumter itself, which has an even longer maritime history than Fort Moultrie. Fort Sumter was nearly in ruins after the Civil War, and was used as an unmanned lighthouse from 1876 to 1897. And in 1898, it was updated and named Battery Huger, though it has never seen combat.

As a historical park, Fort Sumter has no recreational facilities on the grounds, but there's plenty of boating, fishing, kayaking, nature walks, and bird and wildlife viewing nearby.

By the Numbers

231: Acres in the park

1948: Year Fort Sumter was established as a park

5: Number of Fort Sumter's sides and the depth, in feet, of the fort's walls

70,000: Tons of New England granite shipped in to create the foundation of Fort Sumter

2.4: Distance, in miles, a cannonball could travel in 1861

4.5: Distance, in miles, new, improved cannonballs could travel in 1863

34: Hours straight that Confederates fired on the fort on April 12, 1863

1: Indian chief graves, that of Seminole chief Osceola, who died of scarlet fever as a prisoner at Fort Moultrie

RANGER FACT

Fort Sumter had not nearly the number of cannons as had been originally planned in April 1861, due to unwise cutbacks by President James Buchanan, often cited as one of the country's worst presidents.

OTHER NATIONAL PARKS IN

SOUTH CAROLINA

Charles Pinckney
NATIONAL HISTORIC SITE

Congaree NATIONAL PARK

Cowpens NATIONAL BATTLEFIELD

Kings Mountain
NATIONAL MILITARY PARK

Ninety Six NATIONAL HISTORIC SITE

the GREAT AMERICAN BIRDWATCH

PURPLE SANDPIPER

Even in the dead of winter you might catch sight of a Purple Sandpiper scurrying along the sands here—many do not migrate any further south. They are plump, with a white belly and purplish back, and they'll peck along the shorelines for mollusks and other tiny sea creatures.

MOUNT RUSHMORE

NATIONAL MEMORIAL

This is one of the most recognizable American landmarks ever: Presidents George Washington, Thomas Jefferson, Theodore Roosevelt, and Abraham Lincoln gazing across the South Dakota landscape, carved completely from stone by artists and dynamite. Sculptor Gutzon Borglum and his crew began this project in 1927; it was finally finished shortly after his death by his son, Lincoln, in 1941.

If you think working on the mountain sounds like fun, consider this: Workers climbed seven hundred stairs every morning to punch a time clock in windy, blazing hot, and freezing temperatures. They were then suspended by cable over the side of a mountain for the day. The Rocky Mountain goats you may see here would have been better suited to the job!

RANGER FACT

The presidential sculptures were originally supposed to continue down to their waists, but after so many years on the project, money ran out. The final cost: $989,992.32.

There's plenty to see here at Mount Rushmore, from both self-guided and ranger-led tours and visits to the artists' studio to lengthier outdoor evening talks, complete with a film and talk on our nation's history. You can also visit the Lakota, Nakota, and Dakota Heritage Village nearby, and learn about the Native Americans who have lived here for thousands of years.

the GREAT AMERICAN BIRDWATCH

RING-NECKED PHEASANT

South Dakota's state bird is a game bird that has traditionally been one of the most hunted in the world. It is also one of only three birds in the United States that are not native to this country.

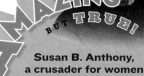

AMAZING BUT TRUE!

Susan B. Anthony, a crusader for women to gain the right to vote, was originally supposed to be the fifth face—and the only woman—on the mountain, until funds ran out. However, her image has been featured on both a postage stamp and a dollar coin!

By the Numbers

1903: Year the park was established

28,291: Acres in the park

600,000+: Visitors annually to the park

4: Approximate number of miles of new cave discovered here each year

70: Top wind speed, measured in miles per hour, at the mouth of the cave

4: Rank of the cave, among caves throughout the world, in terms of length

4–7: Years between fires on the prairie, which keep the small trees from becoming forests

WIND CAVE
NATIONAL PARK

AMAZING BUT TRUE!

Legend has it that when one of the Bingham brothers—who first documented the cave's discovery—looked into the cave's opening, the wind was so strong that it blew his hat off!

Wind Cave is also in the Black Hills, about an hour away from Mount Rushmore, and was the first cave in the world to be declared a national park. Two things are unusual about the cave: the honeycomblike calcite formations inside, called "boxwork," and its sheer size. It is one of the longest and most intricate caves in the world.

Experienced volunteers are constantly exploring Wind Cave: They have charted over 135 miles of passages underground, and are finding more all the time. Visitors can explore the cave, too—there are several different tours available, even one by candlelight.

And keep your eyes open above ground—there are nearly five hundred bison here in the park, roaming on the largest natural-grass prairie in the country.

TAKE A CAVE TRIP THROUGH WIND CAVE

CAVE TEMPERATURE 47° WINTER & SUMMER OPEN ALL THE YEAR

WIND CAVE NATIONAL PARK
U.S. DEPARTMENT OF THE INTERIOR
NATIONAL PARK SERVICE

the GREAT AMERICAN BIRDWATCH

GRAY CATBIRD

The Gray Catbird is a perching bird that gets its name from its talent to mimic. Its call sounds like a cat, but it can also echo the calls of other birds. While its feathers are dull gray in color, its eggs are a surprisingly bright blue. This member of the mockingbird family eats insects, fruits, berries, snails, spiders, and earthworms when the weather warms up.

RANGER FACT

In the 1890s, rumor had it that gold could be found in the cave; when that didn't pan out, the cave began to bring in money in a very unexpected way—tours!

OTHER NATIONAL PARKS In SOUTH DAKOTA

Badlands NATIONAL PARK
Jewel Cave NATIONAL MONUMENT
Minuteman Missile NATIONAL HISTORIC SITE
Missouri NATIONAL RECREATIONAL RIVER

TENNESSEE

NATURALIST SERVICE
SO THAT YOU MAY ENJOY THE GREAT SMOKIES ALL THE MORE

- NATURE WALKS
- ALL DAY HIKES
- LECTURES

A FREE GOVERNMENT SERVICE

GREAT SMOKY MOUNTAINS
NATIONAL PARK..
U.S. DEPARTMENT OF THE INTERIOR

NATIONAL PARK SERVICE ....

MADE BY WPA-CCC

GREAT SMOKY MOUNTAINS
NATIONAL PARK

Bet you wouldn't have guessed: This is the most visited national park in the country! "The Smokies," which is what everyone calls the Great Smoky Mountains, are part of the Blue Ridge Mountains, which are themselves a link in the Appalachian Mountain chain.

The Cherokees were the first inhabitants of these parts, but later on, small towns like Cataloochee, Oconoluftee, Roaring Fork, and Cades Cove sprang up, becoming centers of Appalachian culture. Almost eighty buildings have been preserved, many of them log cabins. With its barns, gristmill, and churches, Cades Cove is the most popular destination in the whole park.

And there's so much else to do here: camping, fly-fishing, biking, horse-back riding, hiking—even part of the famous Appalachian Trail goes through the park. It's so pretty in the Smokies that lots of couples have their wedding right here in the park!

Other great things to experience are the Great Smoky Mountains Institute at Tremont, where kids go to summer camp, and whole families can attend nature workshops and family camp. And the Smoky Mountain Field School offers hikes and adventures for visitors of all ages.

The Smokies are also the place to be to see interesting wildlife, from small to very large: Considered the "Salamander Capital of the World," the Great Smoky Mountains are home to a lungless salamander, which breathes through its skin, and about fifteen hundred black bears!

AMAZING BUT TRUE!

Stealing flowers, or plant poaching, often occurs in the park. There are over sixteen hundred types of wildflowers here. Orchids, trilliums, and ginseng disappear the most.

RANGER FACT

About 95 percent of the park is forest.

the GREAT AMERICAN BIRDWATCH

BLUE-HEADED VIREO

A tiny songbird that loves the woods, the Blue-Headed Vireo has an olive-and-white body, and a grayish, not blue, head. Blue-Headed Vireos feed primarily on the insects they find in the trees of their habitat. They especially love living in a hemlock tree, which may become troublesome over time, as these trees are under attack by an insect called the hemlock wooly adelgid.

OTHER NATIONAL PARKS In TENNESEE

Andrew Johnson
NATIONAL HISTORIC SITE
Big South Fork
NATIONAL RIVER AND RECREATION AREA
Cumberland Gap
NATIONAL HISTORICAL PARK
Fort Donelson
NATIONAL BATTLEFIELD
Obed WILD AND SCENIC RIVER
Stones River NATIONAL BATTLEFIELD

By the Numbers

521,086: Acres in the park (**244,742** in Tennessee; **276,344** in North Carolina)

1934: Year it was established as a park

9,500,000: Approximate number of visitors annually

16: Number of peaks in the park higher than **6,000** feet

1,000: Camp sites over **10** campgrounds

2,115: Miles of streams in the park

1983: Year the park was established

826: Acres in the park

1718: Year the first mission was established

30,000: Approximate number of visitors annually

AMAZING
BUT TRUE!
The churches here are not owned by the national park system—they are still parishes operating under the direction of auspices of the Catholic Archdiocese of San Antonio.

SAN ANTONIO
MISSIONS
NATIONAL HISTORICAL PARK

Photo by Lee Wilder

When we think of what missions are today, we automatically think "church." But that was only part of what a mission was back in the 1700s.

Eighteenth-century missions were entire towns built by the Spanish, who wanted to extend their country's reach from Mexico into what was to become the United States. The goal of these missions was to convert Native Americans into Catholics and make them productive members of Spanish society. Aside from religion, these new communities were also going to be centers to teach farming and ranching.

What's left are the ruins of four famous Texas missions along the San Antonio River: From north to south, they are Mission Concepcion, Mission San José, Mission San Juan, and Mission Espada, including the nearby Espada Aqueduct. The Alamo—Texas' most famous mission—is also nearby, but is not part of the park.

The buildings were completed by 1731. History abounds within them: You may see frescos, or drawings, on the walls that tell a story. Guided tours give visitors insights into the towns, the people, and their livelihood hundreds of years ago. There are concerts and art shows and other events throughout the year—and, of course, lots of armadillos scurrying about. These local

animals can't hear very well, and jump straight up in the air when they're surprised—that's why you often see them as roadkill. They are likely busy chasing the forty thousand ants they can digest in a single day!

SEE AMERICA
UNITED STATES TRAVEL BUREA

MADE BY WORKS PROGRESS ADMINISTRATION · FEDERAL ART PROJECT NYC

ARCHES
NATIONAL PARK

The most famous natural sandstone arch in this park, called the Delicate Arch, is the most often photographed, but there are more than two thousand other arches here to explore! How these stone structures were formed is quite complicated, but a long-ago salt sea and wind joined to make these unusual "sculptures" in the middle of the Utah desert. The names of some of the formations are equally awesome: Fiery Furnace, Devil's Garden, Dark Angel, Devil Dog Spire, and Tower of Babel, to name just a few.

There are tours of the arches and surrounding desert. In addition, camping, backpacking, hiking, and biking are allowed. The park has tried to stop people from climbing some of these famed formations, but clever enthusiasts and some loopholes in park rules seem to win out! Owl Rock is the most popular rock to climb in the park—it's shaped like a totem pole, and it's one hundred feet tall. It takes experts about an hour to reach the top.

RANGER FACT

A prospector and two railroad men brought this scenic wonderland to the attention of the National Park Service after visiting in the early 1920s.

the GREAT AMERICAN BIRDWATCH

RAVEN

The common raven, seen throughout the park, looks very much like a crow. Ravens are quite large, often as long as two feet, with a wingspan that can stretch to five feet. A raven's feathers and beak are black, and these birds will eat just about anything they find. Ravens are also smart birds—scientists have found that they can even solve simple problems.

By the Numbers

1929: Year the park was established as a national monument

76,679: Acres in the park

1,000,000+: Visitors to the park annually

107°F: Highest recorded temperature, in 1989

−14°F: Lowest recorded temperature, in 1989

300: Size, in feet, of the largest arch, named Landscape

AMAZING BUT TRUE!

Arches is located in the high desert. Temperature change can be so radical that it can change 50 degrees in a single day.

By the Numbers

146,597: Acres in the park

1909: Year Zion was established as a park

2,500,000+: Visitors to the park annually

8,726: Highest elevation, in feet, at Horse Ranch Mountain

1917: Year cars begin to visit Zion

15: Length, in miles, of the Zion Canyon (and up to half a mile deep)

19: Species of bats in the park

800: Native species of plants in the park

287: Length in feet, of the Kolob Arch

ZION
NATIONAL PARK
1938

RANGER FACT

Though 271 kinds of birds have been spotted here, only eight types of fish have been found.

ZION
NATIONAL PARK

Like Arches National Park and so many others, we often say Zion National Park was "discovered" by someone or some group. But Native Americans and other humans before them traveled through or lived on these lands for thousands of years before they were "discovered." Still, specifying a date helps us frame it in modern history. In the case of Zion, the Mormons, a religious group that still makes much of Utah their home, discovered Zion Canyon in 1858 and settled here soon after.

Rushing water over a million years has cut through the sandstone to create the park's canyons, one of its most famous features. Canyoneers—people whose passion is climbing in canyons, as opposed to mountain climbers—come from all over the world to experience the beauty here.

If you want to stay on the ground, there are tours and drives so you can experience the spectacular color of this landscape, and trails you can walk that take anywhere from a half-hour to an entire day.

Long ago, wooly mammoths, giant sloths, and camels roamed through here. They're gone now, but you can still spot mountain lions, tarantulas, and plenty of lizards.

AMAZING BUT TRUE!

Over the centuries, there have been many rockslides in the park. About seven thousand years ago, a slide was so big that it created a lake about three miles long and 350 feet deep!

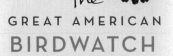

the GREAT AMERICAN BIRDWATCH
PEREGRINE FALCON

When you think of the Peregrine Falcon—a raptor and hunter—you think speed. This bird swoops in on its prey at over two hundred miles per hour, making it the fastest animal on the planet. Mostly it hunts smaller birds, but occasionally it will dive for a rodent or insect. This bluish-gray raptor with a black head can be found almost everywhere except in polar regions.

HIKING TRAILS
HORSEBACK RIDES
MUSEUM EXHIBITS
CAMPFIRE PROGRAMS
NATURE & GEOLOGY TALKS

AMAZING BUT TRUE!

Now Bryce Canyon is also in outer space! In 2007, the International Astronomical Union named the asteroid, formerly called #49272, "Bryce Canyon." It's somewhere between three and five miles wide.

BRYCE CANYON
NATIONAL PARK

BRYCE CANYON NATIONAL PARK
U.S. DEPARTMENT OF THE INTERIOR
EST 1924
NATIONAL PARK SERVICE

If you're a stargazer, this is one of the best places to visit on the entire continent, because it's one of the darkest spots you can find. In some brightly lighted cities, you may only be able to see perhaps a dozen stars, but here, you can see about 7,500—without even using a telescope!

You might think, from the name, that a canyon would be why most people visit. However, it is the amphitheater-like shape of the rock formations—it looks like a natural stadium—that wow visitors. The park encompasses more than six square miles! The shapes cut into the red, orange, and pink rocks are caused by erosion; over millions of years, wind, water, and ice produced this: It's called sedimentary rock. Bring your camera—they say it's almost impossible to take a bad picture here!

Take a scenic ride through the park to see it all, and keep your eyes peeled for mule deer and lots of reptiles, such as the striped whipsnake, the great basin rattlesnake, and the short-horned lizard. But be sure to look for the Utah prairie dog, the smallest of the species and now endangered. They may pop out of one of the little "towns" they build underground.

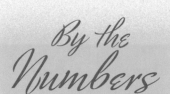

RANGER FACT

The unusual tall, thin, rock formations formed by time and erosion at Bryce Canyon are called *hoodoos*. They change in thickness from top to bottom, and can be as tall as an adult human to higher than a ten-story building.

By the Numbers

1928: Year the park was established

35,835: Acres in the park

2,000,000: Visitors to the park annually

−28°F: Lowest recorded temperature in the park, in 1972

9,100: Highest elevation in the park, in feet

50: Years it takes to erode 1 foot of rock

60: The top speed, in miles per hour, of the park's pronghorn, the second-fastest mammal in the world

CEDAR BREAKS
NATIONAL MONUMENT

By the Numbers

6,155: Acres in the park

1933: Year the park was designated as a monument

600,000+: Visitors annually

3: Distance, in miles, across the canyon

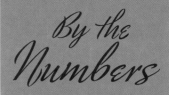

AMAZING BUT TRUE!

Keep your eyes on the trees— you might see some porcupines! The North American variety can climb, and spends lots of time in the branches, searching for food (porcupines even eat bark). Don't worry about one shooting quills at you— that's an old wives' tale.

RANGER FACT

There were awesome rustic lodges built at all the parks in Utah, but the Cedar Breaks Lodge, built in 1924, fell into disrepair and was destroyed in the 1970s. People were so outraged that the National Park Service found a way to keep all the other lodges open.

the GREAT AMERICAN BIRDWATCH

CLARK'S NUTCRACKER

Pine seeds are these birds' favorite food, and they can store about 150 of them at a time in a pouch under their beak.

Though Cedar Breaks is much like Bryce Canyon, with its amphitheater and red rocks, it is at a much higher elevation, so it is often covered in snow from fall to late spring. It sometimes gets up to fifteen feet of the white stuff in winter. That's still a good time to visit, though: you may not see the stunning rock formations, but there's snowshoeing and snowmobiling for fun.

During the summers at Point Supreme Campground, you can see beautiful sunrises and starry night skies—at 10,350 feet above sea level. Then take a hike and check out the famous bristlecone pines: There is one tree here that is sixteen hundred years old. There's also a two-mile loop trail that will lead you through fields of wildflowers or, for the advanced hiker, right outside the park's entrance is Rattlesnake Creek Trail. That's as rugged as it sounds!

OTHER NATIONAL PARKS In UTAH

California NATIONAL HISTORIC TRAIL
Canyonlands NATIONAL PARK
Capitol Reef NATIONAL PARK
Golden Spike NATIONAL HISTORIC SITE
Grand Canyon-Parashant NATIONAL MONUMENT
Hovenweep NATIONAL MONUMENT
Natural Bridges NATIONAL MONUMENT
Timpanogos Cave NATIONAL MONUMENT

SALT RIVER BAY

NATIONAL HISTORICAL PARK AND ECOLOGICAL PRESERVE

On the Caribbean island of Saint Croix is a water park. It's not the kind with slides and waterfalls and chlorine pools, but, rather, a national park designed to save elements of an important marine environment, some of which are threatened and endangered, like its nearby coral reef.

Mangrove forests are found here, too. Mangroves are an important kind of tree found on coasts; their long, twisted root system helps protect shorelines from storm damage, slowing down waves caused by hurricanes and tsunamis. This is a living museum, and nearby there is incredible underwater scenery to be appreciated via scuba diving and snorkeling, and hiking on land.

RANGER FACT

This park is the only known location on U.S. soil where Christopher Columbus's men set foot.

OTHER NATIONAL PARKS In THE VIRGIN ISLANDS

Buck Island Reef
NATIONAL MONUMENT
Christiansted
NATIONAL HISTORIC SITE
Virgin Islands Coral Reef
NATIONAL MONUMENT
Virgin Islands NATIONAL PARK

The GREAT AMERICAN BIRDWATCH

BANANAQUIT
The Bananaquit, seen everywhere on the island, is a small, mostly black bird with a bright yellow belly. Its downward-tipped bill is perfectly shaped for drawing nectar from a flower—the favorite meal of the "sugar bird" (its nickname).

AMAZING BUT TRUE!
The ball court discovered here in 1923 is the only one known to have been built in the Caribbean before Columbus's visit. Games were conducted here for sport—some not so different than those played today.

MARSH-BILLINGS-ROCKEFELLER
NATIONAL HISTORICAL PARK

AMAZING BUT TRUE!

Among his many other talents, George Perkins Marsh was a philologist, which is an expert in the study of languages in literary texts. He knew at least half a dozen European languages and could read and write Scandinavian—but his specialty was Icelandic!

This park was once a farm—a dairy farm, producing milk for Vermonters. It was originally owned by a man named George Perkins Marsh, who was born at the dawn of the nineteenth century. Some call him the first environmentalist, or conservationist.

Born here in Woodstock, he became a lawyer, congressman, and author. Marsh is the first person to speak out against deforestation, or cutting down trees without replanting for further growth. Americans had not yet begun to think about the effects of misusing our resources in the early years of our new nation. In 1864, Marsh even wrote a book about it: *Man and Nature* is one of the first books on saving the environment. Frederick H. Billings, who owned the Northern Pacific Railway and was a fan of Marsh's book, bought the farm in 1864 to put his theories into practice. Billings bought many farms over the years, and began reforesting land. The last owners, the Rockefellers, gave the land to the American people.

The surrounding forests, as well as the gardens here, have been restored for visitors. You can also tour George Marsh's boyhood home and see paintings and photos that influenced the early conservation movement. There are hikes and discussions with rangers about conservation and land stewardship. Trails here are open for hiking and horseback riding, and in the winter for cross-country skiing and snowshoeing.

the GREAT AMERICAN BIRDWATCH

HERMIT THRUSH

The state bird of Vermont, the Hermit Thrush, is just over a foot in length, and mostly brown with a reddish tail. Hermit thrushes live and breed in the forests, so they have George Perkins Marsh to thank for a very woodsy Vermont!

RANGER FACT

Woodstock, Vermont was an important stop on the Underground Railroad before the Civil War, with many townspeople helping slaves escape to freedom in Canada.

By the Numbers

643: Acres in the park

1992: Year established as a park

30,000+: Visitors annually

1: Number of parks devoted to conservation history (this one!)

400: Age in years of some of the hemlocks here

VIRGINIA

AN EASTERN PARK IN THE WESTERN TRADITION

SEE WHITEOAK CANYON FALLS
MOTOR ALONG SKYLINE DRIVE
HIKE THE APPALACHIAN TRAIL

SHENANDOAH
NATIONAL  PARK

U.S. DEPARTMENT
OF THE INTERIOR

EST 1935

NATIONAL PARK
SERVICE

SHENANDOAH
NATIONAL PARK

Shenandoah is a long, skinny park. To its west is the famed Shenandoah River and valley, and the hills of Virginia lie to the east. The most famous part of the park is Skyline Drive, which was built during the Great Depression by the government-sponsored Works Progress Administration (WPA), which provided many jobs for unemployed people during those hard times. The views are spectacular from your car—there are seventy-five overlooks so you can stop and take in the beauty of the rolling hills.

AMAZING BUT TRUE!

Some of the rocks in this park are the oldest in the state, formed more than a billion years ago!

Almost half the land in the park has been set aside as wilderness. So, naturally, hiking is a big attraction. There are more than 500 miles of trails you can walk yourself or with rangers. And not just any trails—101 miles of the famous Appalachian Trail run through Shenandoah. There are great lodges and rustic cabins to stay in if you'd like to spend several days here. Or you can visit Rapidan Camp, which was the vacation home of President Herbert Hoover when he was in the White House from 1929 to 1933 (other presidents liked the idea so much that Camp David was soon built in Maryland as a permanent Washington getaway).

President Hoover came here to fish, and you can, too, plus bike, ride horses, and enjoy all kinds of water sports right outside the park in the Shenandoah River. And there's wildlife everywhere—from thirty-two species of fish to wild turkeys and bears.

By the Numbers

199,017: Acres in the park

1935: Year the park was established

1,000,000+: Visitors annually

105: Length, in miles, of Skyline Drive

35: Speed limit, in miles per hour, on Skyline Drive

862: Species of wildflowers found in the park

93: Height, in feet, of the tallest waterfall, Overall Run

OTHER NATIONAL PARKS In VIRGINIA

Appomattox Court House
NATIONAL HISTORICAL PARK
Arlington House
THE ROBERT E. LEE MEMORIAL
Booker T. Washington
NATIONAL MONUMENT
Cedar Creek and Belle Grove
NATIONAL HISTORICAL PARK
Colonial NATIONAL HISTORICAL PARK
Cumberland Gap
NATIONAL HISTORICAL PARK
Fredericksburg and Spotsylvania County Battlefields Memorial
NATIONAL MILITARY PARK
Fredericksburg NATIONAL CEMETERY
George Washington Birthplace
NATIONAL MONUMENT
George Washington
MEMORIAL PARKWAY
Great Falls PARK
Green Springs NATIONAL HISTORIC LANDMARK DISTRICT
Lyndon Baines Johnson
MEMORIAL GROVE ON THE POTOMAC
Maggie L. Walker
NATIONAL HISTORIC SITE
Manassas
NATIONAL BATTLEFIELD PARK
Petersburg NATIONAL BATTLEFIELD
Prince William Forest PARK
Richmond
NATIONAL BATTLEFIELD PARK
Theodore Roosevelt Island
NATIONAL MEMORIAL
Wolf Trap NATIONAL PARK FOR THE PERFORMING ARTS

WASHINGTON

RANGER NATURALIST SERVICE

HEADQUARTERS PORT ANGELES

VISIT THE RANGER
STATIONS AT

DEER PARK
ELWHA
STORM KING
EAGLE
BOGACHIEL
HOH
QUINAULT
STAIRCASE

FOR INFORMATION ON

WILDERNESS TRAILS
COASTAL RAIN FORESTS
ROOSEVELT ELK
WILDFLOWER MEADOWS
WILDLIFE SANCTUARIES

FOOT AND SADDLE PARTIES WELCOME
ON 390 MILES OF TRAILS

OLYMPIC

NATIONAL PARK

U.S. DEPARTMENT
OF THE INTERIOR

NATIONAL PARK
SERVICE

OLYMPIC

NATIONAL PARK

When pioneers were settling America's West, the Olympic Peninsula was indeed the last frontier. And yet neither white settlers nor Native Americans can claim to be the first inhabitants: Just outside the park's boundaries, the remains of a mastodon were found, with a spear point in its chest. Scientists believe it may be twelve thousand years old!

Olympic National Park, located in the westernmost part of Washington state, has several different regions, due to its sheer size and the fact that it's mountainous, yet borders the Pacific Ocean. It is divided into the Pacific coastline, alpine areas, forests, and a temperate rain forest. Hikers and backpackers like to walk the Ozette Loop, a nine-mile trail along the coast, that is part boardwalk, part beach. Other visitors come to experience the Hoh Rain Forest and the Quinault Rain Forest. This area gets so much rain that it's considered the wettest area in the continental United States. And still more take advantage of the skiing on Hurricane Ridge. As you can see, if you enjoy outdoor sports, it's a full-service park!

Because of the ecological variety of this mammoth park, you'll see all types of animals, from dolphins, whales, seals, and sea otters off the coast, to mountain goats, beavers, cougars, minks, and more on land. After all the camping, fishing, and hiking, you might like to try the Sol Duc Hot Springs, where you can soak in hot mineral and freshwater pools.

RANGER FACT

There is an odd little animal here that you can find only at Olympic—but you may never even see it! The Olympic snow mole tunnels through the deep snow all winter for protection.

By the Numbers

922,650: Acres in the park

1938: Year the park was established

3,000,000: Approximate number of visitors annually

7,980: Height, in feet, of Mount Olympus, the tallest point in the park

0: The lowest point, in feet, in the park, at the Pacific Ocean (sea level)

102°F: Highest recorded temperature, in 1981

150: Inches of rainfall annually in the park's rain forests

the GREAT AMERICAN BIRDWATCH

SOOTY GROUSE

The Sooty Grouse, a Pacific Northwest bird, has mottled gray-brown feathers on its body and head and some plumage that may remind you of a turkey. Sooty Grouses will eat ants, grasshoppers, and other insects, but in colder months they consume greens, berries, and even pine needles.

AMAZING BUT TRUE!

Washington state and Olympic National Park are famous for their salmon that swim hundreds of miles upstream every year to lay their eggs. Many species of this fish are born in a stream, live their lives in the saltwater ocean, and then return once more to freshwater to reproduce.

WASHINGTON

RANGER NATURALIST SERVICE
LONGMIRE   PARADISE VALLEY   YAKIMA PARK   OHANAPECOSH

ILLUSTRATED EVENING
PROGRAMS

NATURE HIKES
AND FIELD TRIPS

MUSEUMS

TRAILSIDE EXHIBITS

NATURE TRAILS

PUBLICATIONS

GENERAL INFORMATION

MOUNT RAINIER
NATIONAL PARK
U.S. DEPT. OF INTERIOR · NATIONAL PARK SERVICE

By the Numbers

235,625: Acres in the park

1899: Year established as a park

2,100,000+: Visitors annually

14,410: Height, in feet, of Mount Rainier

2,500: Approximate number of climbers who reach the summit of Mount Rainer annually, out of the 10,000 people who try

150: Years ago Mount Rainier, an active volcano, last erupted

26: Named glaciers in the park

RANGER FACT

In 2006, a gigantic storm, dubbed the "Pineapple Express," flooded the park so badly that much of it had to be closed for several months. Eighteen inches of rain fell in thirty-six hours!

OTHER NATIONAL PARKS In WASHINGTON

Ebey's Landing
NATIONAL HISTORICAL RESERVE
Fort Vancouver
NATIONAL HISTORIC SITE
Klondike Gold Rush—Seattle Unit
NATIONAL HISTORICAL PARK
Lake Chelan
NATIONAL RECREATION AREA
North Cascades NATIONAL PARK
Ross Lake
NATIONAL RECREATION AREA
San Juan Island
NATIONAL HISTORICAL PARK
Whitman Mission
NATIONAL HISTORIC SITE

MOUNT RAINIER
NATIONAL PARK

Washington's other huge national park also has an amazing centerpiece: Mount Rainier. The highest point in the Cascade Mountain Range, it is also a volcano and the site of many glaciers, including Carbon Glacier, the largest in the United States. There are more than twenty-five other glaciers in the park.

The most popular place to visit is the Paradise Inn, on the south side of Mount Rainier. This rustic lodge, built nearly a century ago, now serves as an inn, a restaurant, and a visitors' center.

The snow on some trails, especially those higher up, doesn't melt until late in the summer. The very highest point you can drive to—at 6,400 feet, and only in the summer months—is called Sunrise, where the first rays of sunshine reach Mount Rainier each day. Not only is there great hiking all through the park, but rangers lead groups on a special snowshoe hike in the winter. For camping and hiking on green, lush forest trails, visit Ohanapecosh. But perhaps the most exciting trail to explore is the ninety-three-mile long Wonderland Trail, which encircles all of Rainier. Some folks hike the whole trail, camping along the way—but know your limits and enjoy what you can!

You may catch a glimpse of a black bear or an elk in the park—but it's the worms, spiders, and insects that are so numerous. They make up about 85% of the creatures here!

AMAZING BUT TRUE!

Mount Rainier is about a million years old, and is considered an active volcano—though it has not erupted since 1894.

> 66 If in the making of the West, Nature had what we call parks in mind—places for rest, inspiration, and prayers—this Rainier region must surely be one of them. 99
>
> —JOHN MUIR

John Brown

Harpers Ferry is quaint and full of history, with museums and exhibits, hiking trails and old-fashioned streets. You might never guess it was the site of one of our country's most historic executions in 1859—the hanging of John Brown.

Brown was an abolitionist, meaning he fought against slavery, which was legal at the time. He and a group of like-minded people attempted to take over the armory in Harpers Ferry so they could give guns to slaves in order to fight against U.S. soldiers. Marines, led by Robert E. Lee, who would soon become a general in the Confederate Army, captured them and hanged Brown. Before his death, John Brown predicted the terrors and bloodshed of the upcoming Civil War. You can visit John Brown's Fort here, right where he fought Robert E. Lee.

But there's even more to Harpers Ferry's history. It was the home to groundbreaking manufacturing during the nineteenth century, with new ideas and inventions that predated the approaching Industrial Revolution. Guns and other military equipment were made here through precision manufacturing, where interchangeable parts can be switched out easily. Even the bullet was developed in this town, replacing slugs. And Harpers Ferry continued to lead the way in civil rights for African-Americans: The famous African-American

civil rights leader and author W.E.B. DuBois held a conference of the Niagara Movement here in 1906. That meeting laid the groundwork for today's National Association for the Advancement of Colored People (NAACP).

Today, you can see Harpers Ferry as it was all those years ago, through museums, events, and talks by rangers and other experts. Plus, you can hike, fish, bike, try white-water rafting, canoeing, visit a wax museum (and see "John Brown" yourself), and even go on a ghost hunting tour in the town of Harpers Ferry, some of which lies outside the park's boundaries.

W.E.B. DuBois

AMAZING
BUT TRUE!

The town of Harpers Ferry changed hands between the North and the South eight times during the Civil War. It's located where the Shenandoah and Potomac Rivers meet, making it a valuable port for both the Union and Confederate armies.

OTHER
NATIONAL PARKS
||||||||||||| In |||||||||||||
WEST VIRGINIA

Appalachian NATIONAL SCENIC TRAIL
Bluestone NATIONAL SCENIC RIVER
Gauley
RIVER NATIONAL RECREATION AREA
New River Gorge NATIONAL RIVER

GREAT AMERICAN *the* BIRDWATCH

CANADA GEESE
You may have seen Canada Geese, flying in formation around dusk, honking their mournful cry. They often meet up at "rest areas" to fly together down South for the winter. The Canada Goose is distinguished from other geese by its black head and neck. Believe it or not, even though they're waterbirds, they mostly eat grain, corn, and, in urban areas, garbage out of trash cans!

HARPERS
FERRY
NATIONAL HISTORICAL PARK

By the Numbers

1944: Year the park was established

2,287.48: Acres in the park

250,000+: Visitors annually

21: Number of men John Brown had in his army

36 ¹/₂: Height, in feet, the Shenandoah and Potomac Rivers rose in a 1936 flood at Harpers Ferry

By the Numbers

1944: Year the park was established

69,372: Acres in the park

175,000: Approximate number of visitors annually

21: Number of Apostle Islands

1 or **2**: Number of times in a century Lake Superior may freeze over entirely

44: Height, in feet, of the Sand House Lighthouse, built in 1921

4: Black bears per square mile on **15.7** square-mile Stockton Island, possibly the densest population in the world

APOSTLE
ISLANDS
NATIONAL LAKESHORE

Here's something a lot of national parks don't offer as recreation: scuba diving for shipwrecks! That's just one of the awesome ways to explore the twenty-one Apostle Islands in Lake Superior, the largest of our Great Lakes. In fact, aside from diving, boating is how you get around these islands, which were formed by glaciers millions of years ago. When the glaciers melted, they left this cluster of islands, made of red sandstone. If you live in the Midwest, you may have even seen a building made of sandstone from one of the Apostle Islands. At the beginning of the twentieth century, much of it was shipped to the Midwest for construction purposes.

the GREAT AMERICAN BIRDWATCH

CLIFF SWALLOW

Elsewhere in the country, you might find a Cliff Swallow nesting under a bridge, a dam, or in a barn rafter; here on the Apostle Islands, the cliff overhangs make perfect homes for these birds. Blue and brown with some white on the throat, this bird mostly eats insects in flight. Mother birds can pick out their own babies' voices, even when they gather in large groups.

RANGER FACT

Though certainly Native Americans, such as the Chippewa, traveled through here, it's thought that fur trappers were the first people who actually settled on the islands, using the money they made from the fur trade to build villages.

Lots of visitors come to see the six lighthouses of the Apostle Islands. To get around, you can take a cruise, bring your own kayak, or travel by boat and tie up at a dock on an island. Be sure to visit the incredible rock formations of the sea caves, which are hollowed-out cliffs and fantastic underground hideaways.

And there's so much more fun to be had: fishing for trout, salmon, and more; camping; hiking; and even hunting. You'll find beaver and tons of small game, but also deer and even, in certain locations, black bear. Oddly enough, some animals that you might normally find on the mainland never made it to the islands, like skunks, raccoons, and chipmunks—guess they can't swim!

OTHER NATIONAL PARKS IN WISCONSIN

Ice Age NATIONAL SCENIC TRAIL
Saint Croix NATIONAL SCENIC RIVER

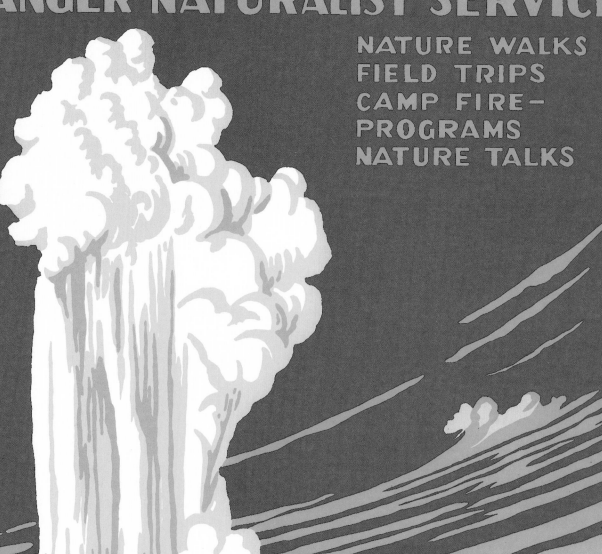

WYOMING

RANGER NATURALIST SERVICE

NATURE WALKS
FIELD TRIPS
CAMP FIRE-
PROGRAMS
NATURE TALKS

YELLOWSTONE
NATIONAL PARK
U.S. DEPARTMENT
OF THE INTERIOR

EST
1872

NATIONAL PARK
SERVICE

YELLOWSTONE
NATIONAL PARK

If you've heard of only one national park, it's probably Yellowstone, the very first national park in the entire world. It's bigger than big—you could fit the states of Delaware and Rhode Island together inside this park!

Among the most astounding things about Yellowstone are the areas where the heat of the Earth is trying to get out. You surely know the most famous of them—Old Faithful! There are as many as ten thousand geysers, hot springs, mud pots, and other thermal features here, more than anywhere else on the planet. These areas are a result of the Yellowstone Caldera, a super-volcano that has had several major eruptions over the last several million years.

AMAZING BUT TRUE!

In the late 1800s, people used Old Faithful as a laundry! Visitors stuffed their dirty clothes into the crater, and when it erupted, the garments came out clean—except that woolens were torn to shreds!

The variety of activities are what makes Yellowstone so special: You can hike, bike, and camp; ride horses out in the backcountry; fish or go boating on Yellowstone Lake; hike with the rangers or sit with them for a campfire program; cross-country ski and or snowmobile in the winter; or simply drive through the park and enjoy its natural splendor.

Yellowstone is famous for its wildlife. Bison, grizzly bears, elk, lynx, wolves, even birds get into the action—ravens have learned how to unzip backpacks and steal! Driving through the park to observe them all (no feeding, please!), stopping for a picnic, and perhaps spending a night at the rustic log hotel, the Old Faithful Inn—this is what a trip to a national park means to most Americans. And it's hard to beat the natural fireworks of Yellowstone's most famous symbol, the spectacular hourly show put on by Old Faithful.

RANGER FACT

Fires are not uncommon in forests, but in 1988 a series of wildfires that burned for several months consumed over 35 percent of the park. At one point over nine thousand firefighters were working to stop them. Today scientists believe that forest fires are part of the natural life and regrowth of nature—as long as they burn far from people and communities.

By the Numbers

1872: Year Yellowstone was designated as a park

2,219,791: Acres in the park

2,000: Earthquakes a year at the park

3,600,000+: Visitors annually

−66°F: Lowest recorded temperature, in 1933

2,400: Miles of streams in the park

22: Number of fires started by lightning each year at the park, 80 percent of which go out naturally

46–92: Minutes between when Old Faithful's eight thousand gallons of water shoot 186 feet into the air

500: Weight, in tons, of the stone fireplace at Old Faithful Inn

30: How fast, in mph, a 2,000-pound bison can run

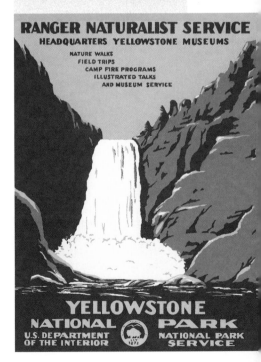

RANGER NATURALIST SERVICE
HEADQUARTERS YELLOWSTONE MUSEUMS

NATURE WALKS
FIELD TRIPS
CAMP FIRE PROGRAMS
ILLUSTRATED TALKS
AND MUSEUM SERVICE

YELLOWSTONE
NATIONAL **PARK**
U.S. DEPARTMENT OF THE INTERIOR   NATIONAL PARK SERVICE

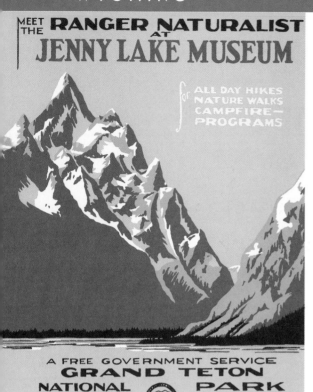

MEET THE **RANGER NATURALIST** AT **JENNY LAKE MUSEUM**

for ALL DAY HIKES
NATURE WALKS
CAMPFIRE—
PROGRAMS

A FREE GOVERNMENT SERVICE
GRAND TETON
NATIONAL 1929 PARK
U.S. DEPARTMENT | NATIONAL PARK
OF THE INTERIOR | SERVICE

GRAND TETON

NATIONAL PARK

You might think of Grand Teton as the little brother of Yellowstone, just ten miles down the road. The two are connected by the John D. Rockefeller Jr. Memorial Parkway—Rockefeller was a very wealthy conservationist who did a lot to ensure the success of this park and several others.

The major star of this park is the Teton Range, a forty-mile stretch of spectacular mountains, the tallest of which is Grand Teton. It's not hard to pick out—it's 850 feet taller than the next highest peak, Mount Owen.

As you can imagine, lots of visitors come here for climbing and mountaineering, but there are countless beautiful spots where you can simply stop and gaze at the local wildlife: Oxbow Bend for trout, osprey, pelicans, and grazing moose and elk; Timbered Island, for the pronghorned antelope, the fastest animal around, which can run up to seventy miles per hour; and Mormon Row to see animals as large as bison and as tiny as grasshoppers, just to name a few. Add to that boating, floating, fishing, horseback riding, biking, and camping, and the nearby ski resorts in Jackson Hole, and you're bound to have fun!

AMAZING BUT **TRUE!**

Wyoming is the least populated of all the fifty states. There are only five people per square mile.

the GREAT AMERICAN **BIRDWATCH**

CALLIOPE HUMMINGBIRD

Isn't it odd that the smallest bird in North America should live in a place so vast! The Calliope Hummingbird weights less than one-tenth of an ounce. Mainly metallic green and white, it has a purplish throat and loves high altitudes. Its long, thin beak is perfect for dipping into nectar.

RANGER FACT

It may not sound new to you, but the Teton Range is the youngest part of the Rocky Mountains, formed six to nine million years ago.

By the Numbers

1929: Year the park was established

310,000: Approximate number of acres in the park

2,500,000: Visitors annually

−63°F: Lowest recorded temperature, in 1933

13,770: Height, in feet, of Grand Teton

100+: Alpine lakes in the park

8: Months in a year Uinta ground squirrels hibernate

180: Inches of snowfall each year in the park

By the Numbers

1906: Year the park was established

1,347: Acres in the park

1,267: Height, in feet, of Devils Tower

430,000+: Visitors annually

1: Percentage of visitors who climb the tower

4–6: Average number of hours it takes to climb Devils Tower

5: Number of people killed attempting to climb Devils Tower

RANGER FACT

Devils Tower's unusual columns are all five-, six-, and seven-sided.

GER NATURALIST SERVICE

⬧ CAMPFIRE PROGRAMS
⬧ WILDLIFE VIEWING
⬧ NATURE WALKS

AMERICA'S FIRST
NATIONAL MONUMENT
DEVILS TOWER
U.S. DEPARTMENT OF THE INTERIOR
NATIONAL PARK SERVICE

DEVILS TOWER
NATIONAL MONUMENT

Does this mountain look familiar? It well might, if you've ever seen the movie *Close Encounters of the Third Kind* (1977), where Devils Tower is the site of an alien landing. You may have thought it was just movie magic, but it's right here in Wyoming!

Nothing looks quite like Devils Tower, and geologists have been studying its formation for years. Most believe it is made of igneous rock, which is formed by cooled lava; its shape may be what's left of the top of a large volcano.

Native American tribes have long considered the tower sacred, and have fascinating tales about how it was formed. Some believe little girls were chased up the mountain by bears, and the unusual columns that form the sides of the mountains are bear-claw marks. In honor of Native American religious beliefs, visitors are asked not to climb Devils Tower in the month of June. But the rest of the year, it is a climbers' paradise, with trails varying from easy to some of the most difficult in the world. Animals that love to nest in crevices make it their homes, such as chipmunks, rock doves, and swallows.

DEVILS TOWER
National 1938 Monument

OTHER
NATIONAL PARKS
In
WYOMING

Bighorn Canyon
NATIONAL RECREATION AREA
Fort Laramie
NATIONAL HISTORIC SITE
Fossil Butte NATIONAL MONUMENT
John D. Rockefeller Jr.
MEMORIAL PARKWAY

the
GREAT AMERICAN
BIRDWATCH

COMMON POORWILL

The Common Poorwill is from the nightjar family and is nocturnal, meaning it comes out at night. The mottled-brown bird has been found hibernating in the desert in the cold, its body temperature low. Where many birds hunt for prey in the air and grab their food as they fly, this bird watches from the ground, then quickly flies to catch moths, beetles, and other insects.

GLOSSARY

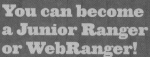

abolitionist Before slavery became illegal in 1865, these people worked to set the slaves free.

alpine Mountains so high that they are above where most vegetation grows, often called the "tree line."

aqueduct A bridgelike structure that carries water over a distance, usually by means of gravity.

bayou A slow-moving body of water, usually a river, found in low-lying lands, especially America's Gulf Coast. Crawfish, shrimp and alligators are often found in these waters.

carrion The body or flesh of dead animals.

deforestation The removal of trees or a complete forest to make way for a different use of the land.

falconry The sport of hunting prey by using trained hawks or falcons.

feral Animals that have not been tamed and are often wild or dangerous.

fissure A narrow opening in the earth, often caused by a shift in the earth over many thousands of years.

geyser A natural hot spring that discharges jets of water and steam into the air.

herbivore An animal that feeds on plants and grass and will not eat meat.

latitude A term used to measure distance north and south around the globe from the equator; longitude measures distances from east to west.

petroglyphs Rock engravings left by ancient peoples that use pictures as language.

philologist A person who studies ancient books and language.

seismograph A machine that measures movement of the ground, especially earthquakes.

shell middens Found on coastlines around the world, these are waste piles of empty mollusk and clam shells left by humans. Some are thousands of years old and several feet high.

stalactite A deposit of minerals, usually spiky in form, that descend from the top of a cave.

stalagmite Deposits from the floor of a limestone cave that form tall spikes; when it meets a stalactite, it forms what's called a column.

Underground Railroad A series of secret routes and safe houses used by American slaves, often with the help of abolitionists, to escape to freedom in either the Northern states or Canada.

You can become a Junior Ranger or WebRanger!

You've visited so many of the country's beautiful national parks with us in this book. Another way to learn more is to become a Junior Ranger or WebRanger. At parks and on the web, the National Park Service has created activities for "kids of all ages" to learn more about specific parks.

JUNIOR RANGER

If you're heading off to one of our great national parks for a visit, check and see if they offer a Junior Ranger program. Go their website (www.nps.gov/learn/junior ranger.cfm) where you'll find links to the many parks that offer the program. If you participate, you'll learn more about the history, nature, art and people of that park and may even earn a Junior Ranger badge or certificate.

WEBRANGERS

You can learn about people, places, history, nature, animals and science, right at home on your computer! You can even design your own Ranger office and print out your very own WebRanger card. Plus, meet other WebRangers just like you! Just go to www.nps.gov/webrangers/ and join now.